Mark Twain on Writing and Publishing

Mark Twain
on Writing and Publishing

Book-of-the-Month Club
New York

This edition was especially created in 1994 for Book-of-the-Month Club.

Compiled by Kathy Kiernan

Printed in the United States of America

CONTENTS

ON WRITING

ON PUBLISHING

On Writing

Comment on Tautology and Grammar

I do not find that the repetition of an important word a few times—say, three or four times—in a paragraph troubles my ear if clearness of meaning is best secured thereby. But tautological repetition which has no justifying object, but merely exposes the fact that the writer's balance at the vocabulary bank has run short and that he is too lazy to replenish it from the thesaurus—that is another matter. It makes me feel like calling the writer to account. It makes me want to remind him that he is not treating himself and his calling with right respect, and, incidentally, that he is not treating me with proper reverence. At breakfast, this morning, a member of the family read aloud an interesting review of a new book about Mr. Gladstone in which the reviewer used the strong adjective "delightful" thirteen times. Thirteen times in a short review, not a long one. In five of the cases the word was distinctly the right one, the exact one, the best one our language can furnish, therefore it made no discord; but in the remaining cases it was out of tune. It sharped or flatted, one or the other, every time, and was as unpleasantly noticeable as is a false note in music. I looked in the thesaurus, and under a single head I found four words which would replace with true notes the false ones uttered by four of the misused "delightfuls"; and of course if I had hunted under related heads for an hour and made an exhaustive search I should have found right words, to a shade, wherewith to replace the remaining delinquents.

I suppose we all have our foibles. I like the exact word, and clarity of statement, and here and there a touch of good grammar for picturesqueness; but that reviewer cares for only the last mentioned of these things. His grammar is foolishly correct, offensively precise. It flaunts itself in the reader's face all along, and struts and smirks and shows off, and is in a dozen ways irritating and disagreeable. To be serious, I write good grammar myself, but not in that spirit, I am thankful to say. That is to say, my grammar is of a high order, though not at the top. Nobody's is. Perfect grammar—persistent, continuous, sustained—is the fourth dimension, so to speak; many have sought it, but none has found it. Even this reviewer, this purist, with all his godless airs, has made two or three slips. At least, I think he has. I am almost sure, by witness of my ear, but cannot be positive, for I know grammar by ear only, not by notes, not by the rules. A generation ago I knew the rules—knew them by heart, word for word, though not their meanings—and I still know one of them; the one which says—which says—but never mind, it will come back to me presently. This reviewer even seems to know (or seems even to know, or seems to know even) how to put the word "even" in the right place; and the word "only," too. I do not like that kind of persons. I never knew one of them that came to any good. A person who is as self-righteous as that will do other things. I know this, because I have noticed it many a time. I would never hesitate to injure that kind of a man if I could. When a man works up his grammar to that altitude, it is a sign. It shows what he will do if he gets a chance; it shows the kind of disposition he has; I have noticed it often. I knew one once that did a lot of things. They stop at nothing.

But, anyway, this grammatical coxcomb's review is interesting, as I said before. And there is one sentence in it which tastes good in the mouth, so perfectly do the last five of its words report a something which we have all felt after sitting long over an absorbing book. The matter referred to is Mr. Gladstone's boswellized conversations and his felicitous handling of his subject.

> One facet of the brilliant talker's mind flashes out on us after another till we tire with interest.

That is clearly stated. We recognize that feeling. In the morning paper I find a sentence of another breed.

> There had been no death before the case of Cornelius Lean which had arisen and terminated in death since the special rules had been drawn up.

By the context I know what it means, but you are without that light and will be sure to get out of it a meaning which the writer of it was not intending to convey.

—1898

The First Writing-Machines

SOME DAYS ago a correspondent sent in an old typewritten sheet, faded by age, containing the following letter over the signature of Mark Twain

> "HARTFORD, MARCH 19, 1875.
>
> Please do not use my name in any way. Please do not even divulge the fact that I own a machine. I have entirely stopped using the typewriter, for the reason that I never could write a letter with it to anybody without receiving a request by return mail that I would not only describe the machine, but state what progress I had made in the use of it, etc., etc. I don't like to write letters, and so I don't want people to know I own this curiosity-breeding little joker.

A note was sent to Mr. Clemens asking him if the letter was genuine and whether he really had a typewriter as long ago as that. Mr. Clemens replied that his best answer is in the following chapter from his unpublished autobiography:

1904. VILLA QUARTO, FLORENCE, JANUARY.

Dictating autobiography to a typewriter is a new experience for me, but it goes very well, and is going to save time and "language"—the kind of language that soothes vexation.

I have dictated to a typewriter before—but not autobiography. Between that experience and the present one there lies a mighty gap—more than thirty years! It is a sort of lifetime. In that wide interval much has happened—to the type-machine as well as to the rest of us. At the beginning of that interval a type-machine was a curiosity. The person who owned one was a curiosity, too. But now it is the other way about: the person who *doesn't* own one is a curiosity. I saw a type-machine for the first time in—what year? I suppose it was 1873—because Nasby was with me at the time, and it was in Boston. We must have been lecturing, or we could not have been in Boston, I take it. I quitted the platform that season.

But never mind about that, it is no matter. Nasby and I saw the machine through a window, and went in to look at it. The salesman explained it to us, showed us samples of its work, and said it could do fifty-seven words a minute—a statement which we frankly confessed that we did not believe. So he put his type-girl to work, and we timed her by the watch. She actually did the fifty-seven in sixty seconds. We were partly convinced, but said it probably couldn't happen again. But it did. We timed the girl over and over again—with the same result always; she won out. She did her work on narrow slips of paper, and we pocketed them as fast as she turned them out to show as curiosities. The price of the machine was one hundred and twenty-five dollars. I bought one, and we went away very much excited.

At the hotel we got out our slips and were a little disappointed to find that they all contained the same words. The girl had economized time and labor by using a formula which she knew by heart. However, we argued—safely enough—that the *first* type-girl must naturally take rank with the first billiard-player: neither of them could be expected to get out of the game any more than a third or a half of what was in it. If the machine survived—*if* it survived—experts would come to the front, by and by, who would double this girl's output without a doubt. They would do one hundred words a minute—my talking speed on the platform. That score has long ago been beaten.

At home I played with the toy, repeating and repeating and repeating "The Boy Stood on the Burning Deck," until I could turn that boy's adventure out at the rate of twelve words a minute; then I resumed the pen, for business, and only worked the machine to astonish inquiring visitors. They carried off many reams of the boy and his burning deck.

By and by I hired a young woman, and did my first dictating (letters, merely), and my last until now. The machine did not do both capitals and lower case (as now), but only capitals. Gothic capitals they were, and sufficiently ugly. I remember the first letter I dictated. It was to Edward Bok, who was a boy then. I was not acquainted with him at that time. His present enterprising spirit is not new—he had it in that early day. He was accumulating autographs, and was not content with mere signatures, he wanted a whole autograph *letter.* I furnished it—in type-machine capitals, *signature and all.* It was long; it was a sermon; it contained advice; also reproaches. I said writing was my *trade,* my bread-and-butter; I said it was not fair to ask a man to give away samples of his trade; would he ask the blacksmith for a horseshoe? would he ask the doctor for a corpse?

Now I come to an important matter—as I regard it. In the year '74 the young woman copied a considerable part of a book of mine *on the machine.* In a previous chapter of this Autobiography I have claimed that I was the first person in the world that ever had a telephone in his house for practical purposes; I will now claim—until dispossessed—that I was the first person in the world to *apply the type-machine to literature.* That book must have been *The Adventures of Tom Sawyer.* I wrote the first half of it in '72, the rest of it in '74. My machinist type-copied a book for me in '74, so I concluded it was that one.

That early machine was full of caprices, full of defects—devilish ones. It had as many immoralities as the machine of to-day has virtues. After a year or two I found that it was degrading my character, so I thought I would give it to Howells. He was reluctant, for he was suspicious of novelties and unfriendly toward them, and he remains so to this day. But I persuaded him. He had great confidence in me, and I got him to believe things about the machine that I did not believe myself. He took it home to Boston, and my morals began to improve, but his have never recovered.

He kept it six months, and then returned it to me. I gave it away twice after that, but it wouldn't stay; it came back. Then I gave it to our coachman, Patrick McAleer, who was very grateful, because he did not know the animal, and thought I was trying to make him wiser and better. As soon as he got wiser and better he traded it to a heretic for a side-saddle which he could not use, and there my knowledge of its history ends.

When a Book Gets Tired

There has never been a time in the past thirty-five years when my literary shipyard hadn't two or more half-finished ships on the ways, neglected and baking in the sun; generally there have been three or four; at present there are five. This has an unbusiness-like look but it was not purposeless, it was intentional. As long as a book would write itself I was a faithful and interested amanuensis and my industry did not flag, but the minute that the book tried to shift to *my* head the labor of contriving its situations, inventing its adventures and conducting its conversations, I put it away and dropped it out of my mind. Then I examined my unfinished properties to see if among them there might not be one whose interest in itself had revived through a couple of years' restful idleness and was ready to take me on again as amanuensis.

It was by accident that I found out that a book is pretty sure to get tired, along about the middle, and refuse to go on with its work until its powers and its interest should have been refreshed by a rest and its depleted stock of raw materials reinforced by lapse of time. It was when I had reached the middle of *Tom Sawyer* that I made this invaluable find. At page 400 of my manuscript the story made a sudden and determined halt and refused to proceed another step. Day after day it still refused. I was disappointed, distressed and immeasurably astonished, for I knew quite well that the tale was not finished and I could not understand why I was not able to go on with it. The reason was very simple—my tank had run dry; it was empty; the stock of materials in it was exhausted; the story could not go on without materials; it could not be wrought out of nothing.

When the manuscript had lain in a pigeonhole two years I took it out one day and read the last chapter that I had written. It was then that I made the great discovery that when the tank runs dry you've only to leave it alone and it will fill up again in time, while you are asleep—also while you are at work at other things and are quite unaware that this unconscious and profitable cerebration is going on. There was plenty of material now, and the book went on and finished itself without any trouble.

Ever since then, when I have been writing a book I have pigeonholed it without misgivings when its tank ran dry, well knowing that it would fill up again without any of my help within the next two or three years, and that then the work of completing it would be simple and easy. *The Prince and the Pauper* struck work in the middle because the tank was dry, and I did not touch it again for two years. A dry interval of two years occurred in *A Connecticut Yankee in King Arthur's Court*. A like interval had occurred in the middle of other books of mine. Two similar intervals have occurred in a story of mine called "Which Was It?" In fact, the second interval has gone considerably over time, for it is now four years since that second one intruded itself. I am sure that the tank is full again now and that I could take up that book and write the other half of it without a break or any lapse of interest—but I shan't do it. The pen is irksome to me. I was born lazy, and dictating has spoiled me. I am quite sure I shall never touch a pen again; therefore that book will remain unfinished—a pity, too, for the idea of it is (actually) new and would spring a handsome surprise upon the reader at the end.

There is another unfinished book, which I should probably entitle "The Refuge of the Derelicts." It is half finished, and will remain so. There is still another one, entitled "The Adventures of a Microbe During Three Thousand Years—by a Microbe." It is half finished and will remain so. There is yet another—*The Mysterious Stranger.* It is more than half finished. I would dearly like to finish it, and it causes me a real pang to reflect that it is not to be. These several tanks are full now, and those books would go gaily along and complete themselves if I would hold the pen, but I am tired of the pen.

There was another of these half-finished stories. I carried it as far as thirty-eight thousand words four years ago, then destroyed it for fear I might some day finish it. Huck Finn was the teller of the story, and of course Tom Sawyer and Jim were the heroes of it. But I believed that that trio had done work enough in this world and were entitled to a permanent rest.

There are some books that refuse to be written. They stand their ground year after year and will not be persuaded. It isn't because the book is not there and worth being written—it is only because the right form for the story does not present itself. There is only one right form for a story, and if you fail to find that form the story will not tell itself. You may try a dozen wrong forms but in each case you will not get very far before you discover that you have not found the right one—then that story will always stop and decline to go any further. In the story of *Joan of Arc* I made six wrong starts, and each time that I offered the result to Mrs. Clemens she responded with the same deadly criticism—silence. She didn't say a word but her silence spoke with the voice of thunder. When at last I found the right form I recognized at once that it was the right one, and I knew what she would say. She said it, without doubt or hesitation.

In the course of twelve years I made six attempts to tell a simple little story which I knew would tell itself in four hours if I could ever find the right starting point. I scored six failures; then one day in London I offered the text of the story to Robert McClure and proposed that he publish that text in the magazine and offer a prize to the person who should tell it best. I became greatly interested and went on talking upon the text for half an hour; then he said, "You have told the story yourself. You have nothing to do but put it on paper just as you have told it."

I recognized that this was true. At the end of four hours it was finished, and quite to my satisfaction. So it took twelve years and four hours to produce that little bit of a story, which I have called "The Death Wafer."

To start right is certainly an essential. I have proved this too many times to doubt it. Twenty-five or thirty years ago I began a story which was to turn upon the marvels of mental telegraphy. A man was to invent a scheme whereby he could synchronize two minds, thousands of miles apart, and enable them to freely converse together through the air without the aid of a wire. Four times I started it in the wrong way and it wouldn't go. Three times I discovered my mistake after writing about a hundred pages. I discovered it the fourth time when I had written four hundred pages—then I gave it up and put the whole thing in the fire.

—1906

Post-Mortem Poetry

In Philadelphia they have a custom which it would be pleasant to see adopted throughout the land. It is that of appending to published death-notices a little verse or two of comforting poetry. Any one who is in the habit of reading the daily Philadelphia *Ledger* must frequently be touched by these plaintive tributes to extinguished worth. In Philadelphia, the departure of a child is a circumstance which is not more surely followed by a burial than by the accustomed solacing poesy in the *Public Ledger.* In that city death loses half its terror because the knowledge of its presence comes thus disguised in the sweet drapery of verse. For instance, in a late *Ledger* I find the following (I change the surname):

DIED

HAWKS.—On the 17th inst., Clara, the daughter of Ephraim and Laura Hawks, aged 21 months and 2 days.

That merry shout no more I hear,
No laughing child I see,
No little arms are round my neck,
No feet upon my knee;

No kisses drop upon my cheek,
These lips are sealed to me.
Dear Lord, how could I give Clara up
To any but to Thee?

A child thus mourned could not die wholly discontented. From the *Ledger* of the same date I make the following extract, merely changing the surname, as before:

> BECKET.—On Sunday morning, 19th inst., John P., infant son of George and Julia Becket, aged 1 year 6 months, and 15 days.
>
> That merry shout no more I hear,
> No laughing child I see,
> No little arms are round my neck,
> No feet upon my knee;
>
> No kisses drop upon my cheek,
> These lips are sealed to me.
> Dear Lord, how could I give Johnnie up
> To any but to Thee?

The similarity of the emotions as produced in the mourners in these two instances is remarkably evidenced by the singular similarity of thought which they experienced, and the surprising coincidence of language used by them to give it expression.

In the same journal, of the same date, I find the following (surname suppressed, as before):

> WAGNER.—On the 10th inst., Ferguson G., the son of William L. and Martha Theresa Wagner, aged 4 weeks and 1 day.
>
> That merry shout no more I hear,
> No laughing child I see,
> No little arms are round my neck,
> No feet upon my knee;
> No kisses drop upon my cheek,

These lips are sealed to me.
Dear Lord, how could I give Ferguson up
To any but to Thee?

It is strange what power the reiteration of an essentially poetical thought has upon one's feelings. When we take up the *Ledger* and read the poetry about little Clara, we feel an unaccountable depression of the spirits. When we drift further down the column and read the poetry about little Johnnie, the depression of spirits acquires an added emphasis, and we experience tangible suffering. When we saunter along down the column further still and read the poetry about little Ferguson, the word torture but vaguely suggests the anguish that rends us.

In the *Ledger* (same copy referred to above) I find the following (I alter surname, as usual):

> WELCH.—On the 5th inst., Mary C. Welch, wife of William B. Welch, and daughter of Catharine and George W. Markland, in the 29th year of her age.

A mother dear, a mother kind,
Has gone and left us all behind.
Cease to weep for tears are vain,
Mother dear is out of pain.

Farewell, husband, children dear,
Serve thy God with filial fear,
And meet me in the land above,
Where all is peace, and joy, and love.

What could be sweeter than that? No collection of salient facts (without reduction to tabular form) could be more succinctly stated than is done in the first stanza by the surviving relatives, and no more concise and comprehensive program of farewells, post-mortuary general orders, etc., could be framed in any form than is done in verse by deceased in the last stanza. These things insensibly make us wiser and tenderer, and better. Another extract:

> BALL.—On the morning of the 15th inst., Mary E., daughter of John and Sarah F. Ball.
>
> 'Tis sweet to rest in lively hope
> That when my change shall come
> Angels will hover round my bed,
> To waft my spirit home.

The following is apparently the customary form for heads of families:

> BURNS.—On the 20th inst., Michael Burns, aged 40 years.
>
> Dearest father, thou hast left us,
> Here thy loss we deeply feel;
> But 'tis God that has bereft us,
> He can all our sorrows heal.
>
> Funeral at 2 o'clock sharp.

There is something very simple and pleasant about the following, which, in Philadelphia, seems to be the usual form for consumptives of long standing. (It deplores four distinct cases in the single copy of the *Ledger* which lies on the Memoranda editorial table):

BROMLEY.—On the 29th inst., of consumption,

Philip Bromley, in the 50th year of his age.

Affliction sore long time he bore,
Physicians were in vain—
Till God at last did hear him mourn,
And eased him of his pain.

The friend whom death from us has torn,
We did not think so soon to part;
An anxious care now sinks the thorn
Still deeper in our bleeding heart.

This beautiful creation loses nothing by repetition. On the contrary, the oftener one sees it in the *Ledger*, the more grand and awe-inspiring it seems. With one more extract I will close:

DOBLE.—On the 4th inst., Samuel Peveril Worthington Doble, aged 4 days.

Our little Sammy's gone,
His tiny spirit's fled;
Our little boy we loved so dear
Lies sleeping with the dead.

A tear within a father's eye,
A mother's aching heart,
Can only tell the agony
How hard it is to part.

Could anything be more plaintive than that, without requiring further concessions of grammar? Could anything be likely to do more toward reconciling deceased to circumstances, and making him willing to go? Perhaps not.

The power of song can hardly be estimated. There is an element about some poetry which is able to make even physical suffering and death cheerful things to contemplate and consummations to be desired. This element is present in the mortuary poetry of Philadelphia degree of development.

The custom I have been treating of is one that should be adopted in all the cities of the land.

It is said that once a man of small consequence died, and the Rev. T. K. Beecher was asked to preach the funeral sermon—a man who abhors the lauding of people, either dead or alive, except in dignified and simple language, and then only for merits which they actually possessed or possess, not merits which they merely ought to have possessed. The friends of the deceased got up a stately funeral. They must have had misgivings that the corpse might not be praised strongly enough, for they prepared some manuscript headings and notes in which nothing was left unsaid on that subject that a fervid imagination and an unabridged dictionary could compile, and these they handed to the minister as he entered the pulpit. They were merely intended as suggestions, and so the friends were filled with consternation when the minister stood up in the pulpit and proceeded to read off the curious odds and ends in ghastly detail and in a loud voice! And their consternation solidified to petrification when he paused at the end, contemplated the multitude reflectively, and then said, impressively:

"The man would be a fool who tried to add anything to that. Let us pray!"

And with the same strict adhesion to truth it can be said that the man would be a fool who tried to add anything to the following transcendent obituary poem. There is something so innocent, so guileless, so complacent, so unearthly serene and self-satisfied about this peerless "hog-wash," that the man must be made to stone who can read it without a dulcet ecstasy creeping along his backbone and quivering in his marrow. There is no need to say that this poem is genuine and in earnest, for its proofs are written all over its face. An ingenious scribbler might imitate it after a fashion, but Shakespeare himself could not counterfeit it. It is noticeable that the country editor who published it did not know that it was a treasure and the most perfect thing of its kind that the storehouses and museums of literature could show. He did not dare to say no to the dread poet—for such a poet must have been something of an apparition—but he just shoveled it into his paper anywhere that came handy, and felt ashamed, and put that disgusted "Published by Request" over it, and hoped that his subscribers would overlook it or not feel an impulse to read it:

(Published by request)

LINES

Composed on the death of Samuel and Catharine Belknap's children

BY M.A. GLAZE

Friends and neighbors all draw near,
    And listen to what I have to say;
And never leave your children dear
    When they are small, and go away.

But always think of that sad fate,
    That happened in year of '63;

Four children with a house did burn,
Think of their awful agony.

Their mother she had gone away,
And left them there alone to stay;
The house took fire and down did burn,
Before their mother did return.

Their piteous cry the neighbors heard,
And then the cry of fire was given;
But, ah! before they could them reach,
Their little spirits had flown to heaven.

Their father he to war had gone,
And on the battle-field was slain;
But little did he think when he went away,
But what on earth they would meet again.

The neighbors often told his wife
Not to leave his children there,
Unless she got some one to stay,
And of the little ones take care.

The oldest he was years not six,
And the youngest only eleven months old,
But often she had left them there alone,
As, by the neighbors, I have been told.

How can she bear to see the place.
Where she so oft has left them there,
Without a single one to look to them,
Or of the little ones to take good care.

Oh, can she look upon the spot,

Whereunder their little burnt bones lay,
But what she thinks she hears them say,
''Twas God had pity, and took us on high.'

And there may she kneel down and pray,
And ask God her to forgive;
And she may lead a different life
While she on earth remains to live.

Her husband and her children too,
God has took from pain and woe.
May she reform and mend her ways,
That she may also to them go.

And when it is God's holy will,
O, may she be prepared
To meet her God and friends in peace,
And leave this world of care.

—1870

Platform Readings

What is called a "reading," as a public platform entertainment, was first essayed by Charles Dickens, I think. He brought the idea with him from England in 1867. He had made it very popular at home and so popular in America that his houses were crowded everywhere, and in a single season he earned two hundred thousand dollars. I heard him once during that season; it was in Steinway Hall, in December, and it made the fortune of my life—not in dollars, I am not thinking of dollars; it made the real fortune of my life in that it made the happiness of my life; on that day I called at the St. Nicholas Hotel to see my *Quaker City* Excursion shipmate, Charley Langdon, and was introduced to a sweet and timid and lovely young girl, his sister. The family went to the Dickens reading, and I accompanied them. It was forty years ago; from that day to this the sister has never been out of my mind nor heart.

Mr. Dickens read scenes from his printed books. From my distance, he was a small and slender figure, rather fancifully dressed, and striking and picturesque in appearance. He wore a black velvet coat with a large and glaring red flower in the buttonhole. He stood under a red upholstered shed behind whose slant was a row of strong lights—just such an arrangement as artists use to concentrate a strong light upon a great picture. Dickens's audience sat in a pleasant twilight, while he performed in the powerful light cast upon him from the concealed lamps. He read with great force and animation, in the lively passages, and with stirring effect. It will be understood that he did not merely read but also acted. His reading of the storm scene in which Steerforth lost his life was so vivid, and so full of energetic action, that his house was carried off its feet, so to speak.

Dickens had set a fashion which others tried to follow, but I do not remember that anyone was any more than temporarily successful in it. The public reading was discarded after a time and was not resumed until something more than twenty years after Dickens had introduced it; then it rose and struggled along for a while in that curious and artless industry called Authors' Readings. When Providence had had enough of that kind of crime the Authors' Readings ceased from troubling and left the world at peace.

Lecturing and reading were quite different things; the lecturer didn't use notes or manuscript or book, but got his lecture by heart and delivered it night after night in the same words during the whole lecture season of four winter months. The lecture field had been a popular one all over the country for many years when I entered it in 1868; it was then at the top of its popularity; in every town there was an organization of citizens who occupied themselves in the off season, every year, in arranging for a course of lectures for the coming winter; they chose their platform people from the Boston Lecture Agency list and they chose according to the town's size and ability to pay the prices. The course usually consisted of eight or ten lectures. All that was wanted was that it should pay expenses; that it should come out with a money balance at the end of the season was not required. Very small towns had to put up with fifty-dollar men and women, with one or two second-class stars at a hundred dollars each as an attraction; big towns employed hundred-dollar men and women altogether, and added John B. Gough, or Henry Ward Beecher, or Anna Dickinson, or Wendell Phillips, as a compelling attraction; large cities employed this whole battery of stars. Anna Dickinson's price was four hundred dollars a night; so was Henry Ward Beecher's; so was Gough's, when he didn't charge five or six hundred. I don't remember Wendell Phillips's price but it was high.

I remained in the lecture field three seasons—long enough to learn the trade; then domesticated myself in my new married estate after a weary life of wandering, and remained under shelter at home for fourteen or fifteen years. Meantime, speculators and money-makers had taken up the business of hiring lecturers, with the idea of getting rich at it. In about five years they killed that industry dead and when I returned to the platform for a season, in 1884, there had been a happy and holy silence for ten years, and a generation had come to the front who knew nothing about lectures and readings and didn't know how to take them nor what to make of them. They were difficult audiences, those untrained squads, and Cable and I had a hard time with them sometimes.

Cable had been scouting the country alone for three years with readings from his novels, and he had been a good reader in the beginning for he had been born with a natural talent for it, but unhappily he prepared himself for his public work by taking lessons from a teacher of elocution, and so by the time he was ready to begin his platform work he was so well and thoroughly educated that he was merely theatrical and artificial and not half as pleasing and entertaining to a house as he had been in the splendid days of his ignorance. I had never tried reading as a trade and I wanted to try it. I hired Major Pond on a percentage to conduct me over the country, and I hired Cable as a helper at six hundred dollars a week and expenses, and we started out on our venture.

It was ghastly! At least in the beginning. I had selected my readings well enough, but had not studied them. I supposed it would only be necessary to do like Dickens—get out on the platform and read from the book. I did that and made a botch of it. Written things are not for speech; their form is literary; they are stiff, inflexible, and will not lend themselves to happy and effective delivery with the tongue—where their purpose is to merely entertain, not instruct; they have to be limbered up, broken up, colloquialized, and turned into common forms of premeditated talk—otherwise they will bore the house, not entertain it. After a week's experience with the book I laid it aside and never carried it to the platform again; but meantime I had memorized those pieces, and in delivering them from the platform they soon transformed themselves into flexible talk, with all their obstructing precisenesses and formalities gone out of them for good.

One of the readings which I used was a part of an extravagant chapter in dialect from *Roughing It* which I entitled "His Grandfather's Old Ram." After I had memorized it it began to undergo changes on the platform and it continued to edit and revise itself, night after night, until by and by, from dreading to begin on it before an audience I came to like it and enjoy it. I never knew how considerable the changes had been when I finished the season's work; I never knew until ten or eleven years later, when I took up that book in a parlor in New York one night to read that chapter to a dozen friends of the two sexes who had asked for it. It *wouldn't read*—that is, it wouldn't read aloud. I struggled along with it for five minutes and then gave it up and said I should have to tell the tale as best I might from memory. It turned out that my memory was equal to the emergency; it reproduced the platform form of the story pretty faithfully, after that interval of years.

The greatest actor would not be able to carry his audience by storm with a book in his hand; reading from the book renders the nicest shadings of delivery impossible. I mean those studied fictions which seem to be the impulse of the moment and which are so effective; such as, for instance, fictitious hesitancies for the right word, fictitious unconscious pauses, fictitious unconscious side remarks, fictitious unconscious embarrassments, fictitious unconscious emphases placed upon the wrong word with a deep intention back of it—these and all the other artful fictive shades which give to a recited tale the captivating naturalness of an impromptu narration can be attempted by a book reader and are attempted, but they are easily detectable as artifice, and although the audience may admire their cleverness and their ingenuity as artifice, they only get at the intellect of the house, they don't get at its heart; and so the reader's success lacks a good deal of being complete.

When a man is reading from a book on the platform, he soon realizes that there is one powerful gun in his battery of artifice that he can't work with an effect proportionate to its caliber: that is the pause—that impressive silence, that eloquent silence, that geometrically progressive silence which often achieves a desired effect where no combination of words howsoever felicitous could accomplish it. The pause is not of much use to the man who is reading from a book because he cannot know what the exact length of it ought to be; he is not the one to determine the measurement—the audience must do that for him. He must perceive by their faces when the pause has reached the proper length, but his eyes are not on the faces, they are on the book; therefore he must determine the proper length of the pause by guess; he cannot guess with exactness and nothing but exactness, absolute exactness, will answer.

The man who recites without the book has all the advantage; when he comes to an old familiar remark in his tale which he has uttered nightly for a hundred nights—a remark preceded or followed by a pause—the faces of the audience tell him when to end the pause. For one audience the pause will be short, for another a little longer, for another a shade longer still; the performer must vary the length of the pause to suit the shades of difference between audiences. These variations of measurement are so slight, so delicate, that they may almost be compared with the shadings achieved by Pratt and Whitney's ingenious machine which measures the five-millionth part of an inch. An audience is that machine's twin; it can measure a pause down to that vanishing fraction.

I used to play with the pause as other children play with a toy. In my recitals, when I went reading around the world for the benefit of Mr. Webster's creditors, I had three or four pieces in which the pauses performed an important part, and I used to lengthen them or shorten them according to the requirements of the case, and I got much pleasure out of the pause when it was accurately measured, and a certain discomfort when it wasn't. In the negro ghost story of "The Golden Arm" one of these pauses occurs just in front of the closing remark. Whenever I got the pause the right length, the remark that followed it was sure of a satisfactorily startling effect, but if the length of the pause was wrong by the five-millionth of an inch, the audience had had time in that infinitesimal fraction of a moment to wake up from its deep concentration in the grisly tale and foresee the climax, and be prepared for it before it burst upon them—and so it fell flat.

In Susy's [Clemens's daughter] little biography of me she tells about my proceeding to tell this ghost tale to the multitude of young lady students at Vassar College—a tale which poor Susy always dreaded—and she tells how this time she gathered her fortitude together and was resolved that she wouldn't be startled, and how all her preparations were of no avail, and how when the climax fell that multitude of girls "jumped as one man"—which is an indication that I had the pause rightly measured that time.

In "His Grandfather's Old Ram" a pause has place; it follows a certain remark, and Mrs. Clemens and Clara, when we were on our way around the world, would afflict themselves with my whole performance every night when there was no sort of necessity for it, in order that they might watch the house when that pause came; they believed that by the effect they could accurately measure the high or low intelligence of the audience. I knew better but it was not in my interest to say so. When the pause was right, the effect was sure; when the pause was wrong in length, by the five-millionth of an inch, the laughter was only mild, never a crash. That passage occurs in "His Grandfather's Old Ram" where the question under discussion is whether the falling of the Irishman on the stranger was an accident, or was a special providence. If it was a special providence, and if the sole purpose of it was to save the Irishman, why was it necessary to sacrifice the stranger? "The dog was there. Why didn't he fall on the dog? Why wa'n't the dog app'inted? Becuz *the dog would 'a' seen him a-comin'.*" That last remark was the one the family waited for. A pause *after* the remark was absolutely necessary with any and all audiences because no man, howsoever intelligent he may be, can instantly adjust his mind to a new and unfamiliar, and yet for a moment or two apparently plausible, logic which recognizes in a dog an instrument too indifferent to pious restraints and too alert in looking out for his own personal interest to be safely depended upon in an emergency requiring self-sacrifice for the benefit of another, even when the command comes from on high.

—1907

A Glimpse at Eve's Diary

Translated From the Original

SATURDAY.—I AM almost a whole day old, now. I arrived yesterday. That is as it seems to me. And it must be so, for if there was a day-before-yesterday I was not there when it happened, or I should remember it. It could be, of course, that it did happen, and that I was not noticing. Very well; I will be very watchful now, and if any day-before-yesterdays happen I will make a note of it. It will be best to start right and not let the record get confused, for some instinct tells me that these details are going to be important to the historian some day. For I feel like an experiment, I feel exactly like an experiment; it would be impossible for a person to feel more like an experiment than I do, and so I am coming to feel convinced that that is what I *am*—an experiment; just an experiment, and nothing more.

Then if I am an experiment, am I the whole of it? No, I think not; I think the rest of it is part of it. I am the main part of it, but I think the rest of it has its share in the matter. Is my position assured, or do I have to watch it and take care of it? The latter, perhaps. Some instinct tells me that eternal vigilance is the price of supremacy. [That is a good phrase, I think, for one so young.]

Everything looks better to-day than it did yesterday. In the rush of finishing up yesterday, the mountains were left in a ragged condition, and some of the plains were so cluttered with rubbish and remnants that the aspects were quite distressing. Noble and beautiful works of art should not be subjected to haste; and this majestic new world is indeed a most noble and beautiful work. And certainly marvelously near to being perfect, notwithstanding the shortness of the time. There are too many stars in some places and not enough in others, but that can be remedied presently, no doubt. The moon got loose last night, and slid down and fell out of the scheme—a very great loss; it breaks my heart to think of it. There isn't another thing among the ornaments and decorations that is comparable to it for beauty and finish. It should have been fastened better. If we can only get it back again—

But of course there is no telling where it went to. And besides, whoever gets it will hide it; I know it because I would do it myself. I believe I can be honest in all other matters, but I already begin to realize that the core and center of my nature is love of the beautiful, a passion for the beautiful, and that it would not be safe to trust me with a moon that belonged to another person and that person didn't know I had it. I could give up a moon that I found in the daytime, because I should be afraid some one was looking; but if I found it in the dark, I am sure I should find some kind of an excuse for not saying anything about it. For I do love moons, they are so pretty and so romantic. I wish we had five or six; I would never go to bed; I should never get tired lying on the moss-bank and looking up at them.

Stars are good, too. I wish I could get some to put in my hair. But I suppose I never can. You would be surprised to find how far off they are, for they do not look it. When they first showed, last night, I tried to knock some down with a pole, but it didn't reach, which astonished me; then I tried clods till I was all tired out, but I never got one. It was because I am left-handed and cannot throw good.

Even when I aimed at the one I wasn't after I couldn't hit the other one, though I did make some close shots, for I saw the black blot of the clod sail right into the midst of the golden clusters forty or fifty times, just barely missing them, and if I could have held out a little longer maybe I could have got one.

So I cried a little, which was natural, I suppose, for one of my age, and after I was rested I got a basket and started for a place on the extreme rim of the circle, where the stars were close to the ground and I could get them with my hands, which would be better, anyway, because I could gather them tenderly then, and not break them. But it was farther than I thought, and at last I had to give it up; I was so tired I couldn't drag my feet another step; and besides, they were sore and hurt me very much.

I couldn't get back home; it was too far and turning cold; but I found some tigers and nestled in among them and was most adorably comfortable, and their breath was sweet and pleasant, because they live on strawberries. I had never seen a tiger before, but I knew them in a minute by the stripes. If I could have one of those skins, it would make a lovely gown.

To-day I am getting better ideas about distances. I was so eager to get hold of every pretty thing that I giddily grabbed for it, sometimes when it was too far off, and sometimes when it was but six inches away but seemed a foot—alas, with thorns between! I learned a lesson; also I made an axiom, all out of my own head—my very first one: *The scratched Experiment shuns the thorn.* I think it is a very good one for one so young.

I followed the other Experiment around, yesterday afternoon, at a distance, to see what it might be for, if I could. But I was not able to make out. I think it is a man. I had never seen a man, but it looked like one, and I feel sure that that is what it is. I realize that I feel more curiosity about it than about any of the other reptiles. If it is a reptile, and I suppose it is; for it has frowsy hair and blue eyes, and looks like a reptile. It has no hips; it tapers like a carrot; when it stands, it spreads itself apart like a derrick; so I think it is a reptile, though it may be architecture.

I was afraid of it at first, and started to run every time it turned around, for I thought it was going to chase me; but by and by I found it was only trying to get away, so after that I was not timid any more, but tracked it along, several hours, about twenty yards behind, which made it nervous and unhappy. At last it was a good deal worried, and climbed a tree. I waited a good while, then gave it up and went home.

To-day the same thing over. I've got it up the tree again.

SUNDAY.—It is up there yet. Resting, apparently. But that is a subterfuge: Sunday isn't the day of rest; Saturday is appointed for that. It looks to me like a creature that is more interested in resting than in anything else. It would tire me to rest so much. It tires me just to sit around and watch the tree. I do wonder what it is for; I never see it do anything.

They returned the moon last night, and I was so happy! I think it is very honest of them. It slid down and fell off again, but I was not distressed; there is no need to worry when one has that kind of neighbors; they will fetch it back. I wish I could do something to show my appreciation. I would like to send them some stars, for we have more than we can use. I mean I, not we, for I can see that the reptile cares nothing for such things.

It has low tastes, and is not kind. When I went there

yesterday evening in the gloaming it had crept down and was trying to catch the little speckled fishes that play in the pool, and I had to clod it to make it go up the tree again and let them alone. I wonder if *that* is what it is for? Hasn't it any heart? Hasn't it any compassion for those little creatures? Can it be that it was designed and manufactured for such ungentle work? It has the look of it. One of the clods took it back of the ear, and it used language. It gave me a thrill, for it was the first time I had ever heard speech, except my own. I did not understand the words, but they seemed expressive.

When I found it could talk I felt a new interest in it, for I love to talk; I talk, all day, and in my sleep, too, and I am very interesting, but if I had another to talk to I could be twice as interesting, and would never stop, if desired.

If this reptile is a man, it isn't an *it*, is it? That wouldn't be grammatical, would it? I think it would be *he*. I think so. In that case one would parse it thus: nominative, *he*; dative, *him*; possessive, *his'n*. Well, I will consider it a man and call it he until it turns out to be something else. This will be handier than having so many uncertainties.

NEXT WEEK SUNDAY.—All the week I tagged around after him and tried to get acquainted. I had to do the talking, because he was shy, but I didn't mind it. He seemed pleased to have me around, and I used the sociable "we" a good deal, because it seemed to flatter him to be included.

WEDNESDAY.—We are getting along very well indeed, now, and getting better and better acquainted. He does not try to avoid me any more, which is a good sign, and shows that he likes to have me with him. That pleases me, and I study to be useful to him in every way I can, so as to increase his regard. During the last day or two I have taken all the work of naming things off his hands, and this has been a great relief to him, for he has not gift in that line, and is evidently very grateful. He can't think of a rational name to save him, but I do not let him see that I am aware of his defect. Whenever a new creature comes along I name it before he has time to expose himself by an awkward silence. In this way I have saved him many embarrassments. I have no defect like his. The minute I set eyes on an animal I know what it is. I don't have to reflect a moment; the right name comes out instantly, just as if it were an inspiration, as no doubt it is, for I am sure it wasn't in me half a minute before. I seem to know just by the shape of the creature and the way it acts what animal it is.

When the dodo came along he thought it was a wildcat—I saw it in his eye. But I saved him. And I was careful not to do it in a way that could hurt his pride. I just spoke up in a quite natural way of pleased surprise, and not as if I was dreaming of conveying information, and said, "Well, I do declare, if there isn't the dodo!" I explained—without seeming to be explaining—how I knew it for a dodo, and although I thought maybe he was a little piqued that I knew the creature when he didn't, it was quite evident that he admired me. That was very agreeable, and I thought of it more than once with gratification before I slept. How little a thing can make us happy when we feel that we have earned it!

THURSDAY.—My first sorrow. Yesterday he avoided me and seemed to wish I would not talk to him. I could not believe it, and thought there was some mistake, for I loved to be with him, and loved to hear him talk, and so how could it be that he could feel unkind toward me when I had not done anything? But at last it seemed true, so I went away and sat lonely in the place where I first saw him the morning that we were made and I did not know what he was and was indifferent about him; but now it was a mournful place, and every little thing spoke of him, and my heart was very sore. I did not know why very clearly, for it was a new feeling; I had not experienced it before, and it was all a mystery, and I could not make it out.

But when night came I could not bear the lonesomeness, and went to the new shelter which he has built, to ask him what I had done that was wrong and how I could mend it and get back his kindness again; but he put me out in the rain, and it was my first sorrow.

SUNDAY.—It is pleasant again, now, and I am happy; but those were heavy days; I do not think of them when I can help it.

I tried to get him some of those apples, but I cannot learn to throw straight. I failed, but I think the good intention pleased him. They are forbidden, and he says I shall come to harm; but so I come to harm through pleasing him, why shall I care for that harm?

MONDAY.—This morning I told him my name, hoping it would interest him. But he did not care for it. It is strange. If he should tell me his name, I would care. I think it would be pleasanter in my ears than any other sound.

He talks very little. Perhaps it is because he is not bright, and is sensitive about it and wishes to conceal it. It is such a pity that he should feel so, for brightness is nothing; it is in the heart that the values lie. I wish I could make him understand that a loving good heart is riches, and riches enough, and that without it intellect is poverty.

Although he talks so little, he has quite a considerable vocabulary. This morning he used a surprisingly good word. He evidently recognized, himself, that it was a good one, for he worked it in twice afterward, casually. It was not good casual art, still it showed that he possesses a certain quality of perception. Without a doubt that seed can be made to grow, if cultivated.

Where did he get that word? I don't think I have ever used it.

No, he took no interest in my name. I tried to hide my disappointment, but I suppose I did not succeed. I went away and sat on the moss-bank with my feet in the water. It is where I go when I hunger for companionship, some one to look at, some one to talk to. It is not enough—that lovely white body painted there in the pool—but it is something, and something is better than utter loneliness. It talks when I talk; it is sad when I am sad; it comforts me with its sympathy; it says, "Do not be downhearted, you poor friendless girl; I will be your friend." It *is* a good friend to me, and my only one; it is my sister.

That first time that she forsook me! ah, I shall never forget that—never, never. My heart was lead in my body! I said, "She was all I had, and now she is gone!" In my despair I said, "Break, my heart; I cannot bear my life any more!" and hid my face in my hands, and there was no solace for me. And when I took them away, after a little, there she was again, white and shining and beautiful, and I sprang into her arms!

That was perfect happiness; I had known happiness before, but it was not like this, which was ecstasy. I never doubted her afterward. Sometimes she stayed away—maybe an hour, maybe almost the whole day, but I waited and did not doubt; I said, "She is busy, or she is gone a journey, but she will come." And it was so: she always did. At night she would not come if it was dark, for she was a timid little thing; but if there was a moon she would come.

I am not afraid of the dark, but she is younger than I am; she was born after I was. Many and many are the visits I have paid her; she is my comfort and my refuge when my life is hard—and it is mainly that.

TUESDAY.—All the morning I was at work improving the estate; and I purposely kept away from him in the hope that he would get lonely and come. But he did not.

At noon I stopped for the day and took my recreation by flitting all about with the bees and the butterflies and reveling in the flowers, those beautiful creatures that catch the smile of God out of the sky and preserve it! I gathered them, and made them into wreaths and garlands and clothed myself in them while I ate my luncheon—apples, of course; then I sat in the shade and wished and waited. But he did not come.

But no matter. Nothing would have come of it, for he does not care for flowers. He calls them rubbish, and cannot tell one from another, and thinks it is superior to feel like that. He does not care for me, he does not care for flowers, he does not care for the painted sky at eventide—is there anything he does care for, except building shacks to coop himself up in from the good clean rain, and thumping the melons, and sampling the grapes, and fingering the fruit on the trees, to see how those properties are coming along?

I laid a dry stick on the ground and tried to bore a hole in it with another one, in order to carry out a scheme that I had, and soon I got an awful fright. A thin, transparent bluish film rose out of the hole, and I dropped everything and ran! I thought it was a spirit, and I was so frightened! But I looked back, and it was not coming; so I leaned against a rock and rested and panted, and let my limbs go on trembling until they got steady again; then I crept warily back, alert, watching, and ready to fly if there was occasion; and when I was come near, I parted the branches of a rose-bush and peeped through—wishing the man was about, I was looking so cunning and pretty—but the sprite was gone. I went there, and there was a pinch of delicate pink dust in the hole. I put my finger in, to feel it, and said *ouch!* and took it out again. It was a cruel pain. I put my finger in my mouth; and by standing first on one foot and then the other, and grunting, I presently eased my misery; then I was full of interest, and began to examine.

I was curious to know what the pink dust was. Suddenly the name of it occurred to me, though I had never heard of it before. It was *fire*! I was as certain of it as a person could be of anything in the world. So without hesitation I named it that—fire.

I had created something that didn't exist before; I had added a new thing to the world's uncountable properties; I realized this, and was proud of my achievement, and was going to run and find him and tell him about it, thinking to raise myself in his esteem—but I reflected, and did not do it. No—he would not care for it. He would ask what it was good for, and what could I answer? For if it was not *good* for something, but only beautiful, merely beautiful—

So I sighed, and did not go. For it wasn't good for anything; it could not build a shack, it could not improve melons, it could not hurry a fruit crop; it was useless, it was a foolishness and a vanity; he would despise it and say cutting words. But to me it was not despicable; I said, "Oh, you fire, I love you, you dainty pink creature, for you are *beautiful*—and that is enough!" and was going to gather it to my breast. But refrained. Then I made another maxim out of my own head, though it was so nearly like the first one that I was afraid it was only a plagiarism: "*The burnt Experiment shuns the fire.*"

I wrought again; and when I had made a good deal of fire-dust I emptied it into a handful of dry brown grass, intending to carry it home and keep it always and play with it; but the wind struck it and it sprayed up and spat out at me fiercely, and I dropped it and ran. When I looked back the blue spirit was towering up and stretching and rolling away like a cloud, and instantly I thought of the name of it—*smoke!*—though, upon my word, I had never heard of smoke before.

Soon, brilliant yellow and red flares shot up through the smoke, and I named them in an instant—*flames*—I was right, too, though these were the very first flames that had ever been in the world. They climbed the trees, they flashed splendidly in and out of the vast and increasing volume of tumbling smoke, and I had to clap my hands and laugh and dance in my rapture, it was so new and strange and so wonderful and so beautiful!

He came running, and stopped and gazed, and said not a word for many minutes. Then he asked what it was. Ah, it was too bad that he should ask such a direct question. I had to answer it, of course, and I did. I said it was fire. If it annoyed him that I should know and he must ask; that was not my fault; I had no desire to annoy him. After a pause he asked:

"How did it come?"

Another direct question, and it also had to have a direct answer.

"I made it."

The fire was traveling farther and farther off. He went to the edge of the burned place and stood looking down, and said:

"What are these?"

"Fire-coals."

He picked up one to examine it, but changed his mind

and put it down again. Then he went away. *Nothing* interests him.

But I was interested. There were ashes, gray and soft and delicate and pretty—I knew what they were at once. And the embers; I knew the embers, too. I found my apples, and raked them out, and was glad; for I am very young and my appetite is active. But I was disappointed; they were all burst open and spoiled. Spoiled apparently; but it was not so; they were better than raw ones. Fire is beautiful; some day it will be useful, I think.

FRIDAY.—I saw him again, for a moment, last Monday at nightfall, but only for a moment. I was hoping he would praise me for trying to improve the estate, for I had meant well and had worked hard. But he was not pleased, and turned away and left me. He was also displeased on another account: I tried once more to persuade him to stop going over the Falls. That was because the fire had revealed to me a new passion—quite new, and distinctly different from love, grief, and those others which I had already discovered—*fear*. And it is horrible!—I wish I had never discovered it; it gives me dark moments, it spoils my happiness, it makes me shiver and tremble and shudder. But I could not persuade him, or he has not discovered fear yet, and so he could not understand me.

EXTRACT FROM ADAM'S DIARY

Perhaps I ought to remember that she is very young, a mere girl, and make allowances. She is all interest, eagerness, vivacity, the world is to her a charm, a wonder, a mystery, a joy; she can't speak for delight when she finds a new flower, she must pet it and caress it and smell it and talk to it, and pour out endearing names upon it. And she is color-mad: brown rocks, yellow sand, gray moss, green foliage, blue sky; the pearl of the dawn, the purple shadows on the mountains, the golden islands floating in crimson seas at sunset, the pallid moon sailing through the shredded cloud-rack, the star-jewels glittering in the wastes of space—none of them is of any practical value, so far as I can see, but because they have color and majesty, that is enough for her, and she loses her mind over them. If she could quiet down and keep still a couple of minutes at a time, it would be a reposeful spectacle. In that case I think I could enjoy looking at her; indeed I am sure I could, for I am coming to realize that she is a quite remarkably comely creature—lithe, slender, trim, rounded, shapely, nimble, graceful; and once when she was standing marble-white and sun-drenched on a boulder, with her young head tilted back and her hand shading her eyes, watching the flight of a bird in the sky, I recognized that she was beautiful.

MONDAY NOON.—*If there is anything on the planet that she is not interested in it is not in my list. There are animals that I am indifferent to, but it is not so with her. She has no discrimination, she takes to all of them, she thinks they are all treasures, every new one is welcome.*

When the mighty brontosaurus came striding into camp, she regarded it as an acquisition, I considered it a calamity; that is a good sample of the lack of harmony that prevails in our views of things. She wanted to domesticate it, I wanted to make it a present of the homestead and move out. She believed it could be tamed by kind treatment and would be a good pet; I said a pet twenty-one feet high and eighty-four feet long would be no proper thing to have about the place, because, even with the best intentions and without meaning any harm, it could sit down on the house and mash it, for any one could see by the look of its eye that it was absent-minded.

Still, her heart was set upon having that monster, and she couldn't give it up. She thought we could start a dairy with it, and wanted me to help her milk it; but I wouldn't; it was too risky. The sex wasn't right, and we hadn't any ladder anyway. Then she wanted to ride it, and look at the scenery. Thirty or forty feet of its tail was lying on the ground, like a fallen tree, and she thought she could climb it, but she was mistaken; when she got to the steep place it was too slick and down she came, and would have hurt herself but for me.

Was she satisfied now? No. Nothing ever satisfies her but demonstration; untested theories are not in her line, and she won't have them. It is the right spirit, I concede it; it attracts me; I feel the influence of it; if I were with her more I think I should take it up myself. Well, she had one theory remaining about this colossus; she thought that if we could tame him and make him friendly we could stand him in the river and use him for a bridge. It turned out that he was already plenty tame enough—at least as far as she was concerned—so she tried her theory, but it failed; every time she got him properly placed in the river and went ashore to cross over on him, he came out and followed her around like a pet mountain. Like the other animals. They all do that.

FRIDAY.—Tuesday—Wednesday—Thursday—and today: all without seeing him. It is a long time to be alone; still, it is better to be alone than unwelcome.

I *had* to have company—I was made for it, I think—so I made friends with the animals. They are just charming, and they have the kindest disposition and the politest ways; they never look sour, they never let you feel that you are intruding, they smile at you and wag their tail, if they've got one, and they are always ready for a romp or an excursion or anything you want to propose. I think they are perfect gentlemen. All these days we have had such good times, and it hasn't been lonesome for me, ever. Lonesome! No, I should say not. Why, there's always a swarm of them around—sometimes as much as four or five acres—you can't count them; and when you stand on a rock in the midst and look out over the furry expanse it is so mottled and splashed and gay with color and frisking sheen and sun-flash, and so rippled with stripes, that you might think it was a lake, only you know it isn't; and there's storms of sociable birds, and hurricanes of whirring wings; and when the sun strikes all that feathery commotion, you have a blazing up of all the colors you can think of, enough to put your eyes out.

We have made long excursions, and I have seen a great deal of the world; almost all of it, I think; and so I am the first traveler, and the only one. When we are on the march, it is an imposing sight—there's nothing like it anywhere. For comfort I ride a tiger or a leopard, because it is soft and has a round back that fits me, and because they are such pretty animals; but for long distance or for scenery I ride the elephant. He hoists me up with his trunk, but I can get off myself; when we are ready to camp, he sits and I slide down the back way.

The birds and animals are all friendly to each other, and there are no disputes about anything. They all talk, and they all talk to me, but it must be a foreign language, for I cannot make out a word they say; yet they often understand me when I talk back, particularly the dog and the elephant. It makes me ashamed. It shows that they are brighter than I am, and are therefore my superiors. It annoys me, for I want to be the principal Experiment myself—and I intend to be, too.

I have learned a number of things, and am educated, now, but I wasn't at first. I was ignorant at first. At first it used to vex me because, with all my watching, I was never smart enough to be around when the water was running uphill; but now I do not mind it. I have experimented and experimented until now I know it never does run uphill, except in the dark. I know it does in the dark, because the pool never goes dry, which it would, of course, if the water didn't come back in the night. It is best to prove things by actual experiment; then you *know;* whereas if you depend on guessing and supposing and conjecturing, you will never get educated.

Some things you *can't* find out; but you will never know you can't by guessing and supposing: no, you have to be patient and go on experimenting until you find out that you can't find out. And it is delightful to have it that way, it makes the world so interesting. If there wasn't anything to find out, it would be dull. Even trying to find out and not finding out is just as interesting as trying to find out and finding out, and I don't know but more so. The secret of the water was a treasure until I *got* it; then the excitement all went away, and I recognized a sense of loss.

By experiment I know that wood swims, and dry leaves, and feathers, and plenty of other things; therefore by all that cumulative evidence you know that a rock will swim; but you have to put up with simply knowing it, for there isn't any way to prove it—up to now. But I shall find a way—then *that* excitement will go. Such things make me sad; because by and by when I have found out everything there won't be any more excitements, and I do love excitements so! The other night I couldn't sleep for thinking about it.

At first I couldn't make out what I was made for, but now I think it was to search out the secrets of this wonderful world and be happy and thank the Giver of it all for devising it. I think there are many things to learn yet—I hope so; and by economizing and not hurrying too fast I think they will last weeks and weeks. I hope so. When you cast up a feather it sails away on the air and goes out of sight; then you throw up a clod and it doesn't. It comes down, every time. I have tried it and tried it, and it is always so. I wonder why it is? Of course it *doesn't* come down, but why should it *seem* to? I suppose it is an optical illusion. I mean, one of them is. I don't know which one. It may be the feather, it may be the clod; I can't prove which it is, I can only demonstrate that one or the other is a fake, and let a person take his choice.

By watching, I know that the stars are not going to last. I have seen some of the best ones melt and run down the sky. Since one can melt, they can all melt; since they can all melt, they can all melt the same night. That sorrow will come—I know it. I mean to sit up every night and look at them as long as I can keep awake; and I will impress those sparkling fields on my memory, so that by and by when they are taken away I can by my fancy restore those lovely myriads to the black sky and make them sparkle again, and double them by the blur of my tears.

After the Fall

When I look back, the Garden is a dream to me. It was beautiful, surpassingly beautiful, enchantingly beautiful; and now it is lost, and I shall not see it any more.

The Garden is lost, but I have found *him,* and am content. He loves me as well as he can; I love him with all the strength of my passionate nature, and this, I think, is proper to my youth and sex. If I ask myself why I love him, I find I do not know, and do not really much care to know; so I suppose that this kind of love is not a product of reasoning and statistics, like one's love for other reptiles and animals. I think that this must be so. I love certain birds because of their song; but I do not love Adam on account of his singing—no, it is not that; the more he sings the more I do not get reconciled to it. Yet I ask him to sing, because I wish to learn to like everything he is interested in. I am sure I can learn, because at first I could not stand it, but now I can. It sours the milk, but it doesn't matter; I can get used to that kind of milk.

It is not on account of his brightness that I love him—no, it is not that. He is not to blame for his brightness, such as it is, for he did not make it himself; he is as God made him, and that is sufficient. There was a wise purpose in it, *that* I know. In time it will develop, though I think it will not be sudden; and besides, there is no hurry; he is well enough just as he is.

It is not on account of his gracious and considerate ways and his delicacy that I love him. No, he has lacks in these regards, but he is well enough just so, and is improving.

It is not on account of his industry that I love him—no, it is not that. I think he has it in him, and I do not know why he conceals it from me. It is my only pain. Otherwise he is frank and open with me, now. I am sure he keeps nothing from me but this. It grieves me that he should have a secret from me, and sometimes it spoils my sleep, thinking of it, but I will put it out of my mind; it shall not trouble my happiness, which is otherwise full to overflowing.

It is not on account of his education that I love him—no, it is not that. He is self-educated, and does really know a multitude of things, but they are not so.

It is not on account of his chivalry that I love him—no, it is not that. He told on me, but I do not blame him; it is a peculiarity of sex, I think, and he did not make his sex. Of course I would not have told on him, I would have perished first; but that is a peculiarity of sex, too, and I do not take credit for it, for I did not make my sex.

Then why is it that I love him? *Merely because he is masculine, I think.*

At bottom he is good, and I love him for that, but I could love him without it. If he should beat me and abuse me, I should go on loving him. I know it. It is a matter of sex, I think.

He is strong and handsome, and I love him for that, and I admire him and am proud of him, but I could love him without those qualities. If he were plain, I should love him; if he were a wreck, I should love him; and I would work for him, and slave over him, and pray for him, and watch by his bedside until I died.

Yes, I think I love him merely because he is *mine* and is *masculine*. There is no other reason, I suppose. And so I think it is as I first said: that this kind of love is not a product of reasonings and statistics. It just *comes*—none knows whence—and cannot explain itself. And doesn't need to.

It is what I think. But I am only a girl, and the first that has examined this matter, and it may turn out that in my ignorance and inexperience I have not got it right.

Forty Years Later

It is my prayer, it is my longing, that we may pass from this life together—a longing which shall never perish from the earth, but shall have place in the heart of every wife that loves, until the end of time; and it shall be called by my name.

But if one of us must go first, it is my prayer that it shall be I; for he is strong, I am weak, I am not so necessary to him as he is to me—life without him would not be life; how could I endure it? This prayer is also immortal, and will not cease from being offered up while my race continues. I am the first wife; and in the last wife I shall be repeated.

At Eve's Grave

Adam: Wheresoever she was, *there* was Eden.

THE END

On Writers

Rudyard Kipling

This morning's cables contain a verse or two from Kipling, voicing his protest against a liberalizing new policy of the British government which he fears will deliver the balance of power in South Africa into the hands of the conquered Boers. Kipling's name, and Kipling's words always stir me now, stir me more than do any other living man's. But I remember a time, seventeen or eighteen years back, when the name did not suggest anything to me and only the words moved me. At that time Kipling's name was beginning to be known here and there, in spots, in India, but had not traveled outside of that empire. He came over and traveled about America, maintaining himself by correspondence with Indian journals. He wrote dashing, free-handed, brilliant letters but no one outside of India knew about it.

On his way through the State of New York he stopped off at Elmira and made a tedious and blistering journey up to Quarry Farm in quest of me. He ought to have telephoned the farm first; then he would have learned that I was at the Langdon homestead, hardly a quarter of a mile from his hotel. But he was only a lad of twenty-four and properly impulsive and he set out without inquiring on that dusty and roasting journey up the hill. He found Susy Crane and my little Susy there, and they came as near making him comfortable as the weather and the circumstances would permit.

The group sat on the veranda and while Kipling rested and refreshed himself he refreshed the others with his talk, talk of a quality which was well above what they were accustomed to, talk which might be likened to footprints, so strong and definite was the impression which it left behind. They often spoke wonderingly of Kipling's talk afterward, and they recognized that they had been in contact with an extraordinary man, but it is more than likely that they were the only persons who had perceived that he was extraordinary. It is not likely that they perceived his full magnitude, it is most likely that they were Eric Ericsons who had discovered a continent but did not suspect the horizonless extent of it. His was an unknown name and was to remain unknown for a year yet, but Susy kept his card and treasured it as an interesting possession. Its address was Allahabad.

No doubt India had been to her an imaginary land up to this time, a fairyland, a dreamland, a land made out of poetry and moonlight for the Arabian Nights to do their gorgeous miracles in; and doubtless Kipling's flesh and blood and modern clothes realized it to her for the first time and solidified it. I think so because she more than once remarked upon its incredible remoteness from the world that we were living in, and computed that remoteness and pronounced the result with a sort of awe, fourteen thousand miles, or sixteen thousand, whichever it was. Kipling had written upon the card a compliment to me. This gave the card an additional value in Susy's eyes, since as a distinction it was the next thing to being recognized by a denizen of the moon.

Kipling came down that afternoon and spent a couple

of hours with me, and at the end of that time I had surprised him as much as he had surprised me, and the honors were easy. I believed that he knew more than any person I had met before, and I knew that he knew I knew less than any person he had met before—though he did not say it and I was not expecting that he would. When he was gone, Mrs. Langdon wanted to know about my visitor. I said, "He is a stranger to me but he is a most remarkable man—and I am the other one. Between us, we cover all knowledge; he knows all that can be known, and I know the rest."

He was a stranger to me and to all the world, and remained so for twelve months, then he became suddenly known and universally known. From that day to this he has held this unique distinction: that of being the only living person, not head of a nation, whose voice is heard around the world the moment it drips a remark, the only such voice in existence that does not go by slow ship and rail but always travels first-class by cable.

About a year after Kipling's visit in Elmira, George Warner came into our library one morning in Hartford, with a small book in his hand, and asked me if I had ever heard of Rudyard Kipling. I said, "No."

He said I would hear of him very soon, and that the noise he was going to make would be loud and continuous. The little book was the *Plain Tales* and he left it for me to read, saying it was charged with a new and inspiriting fragrance and would blow a refreshing breath around the world that would revive the nations. A day or two later he brought a copy of the London *World* which had a sketch of Kipling in it, and a mention of that fact that he had traveled in the United States. According to this sketch he had passed through Elmira. This remark, added to the additional fact that he hailed from India, attracted my attention—also Susy's. She went to her room and brought his card from its place in the frame of her mirror, and the Quarry Farm visitor stood identified.

I am not acquainted with my own books but I know Kipling's—at any rate I know them better than I know anybody else's books. They never grow pale to me; they keep their color; they are always fresh. Certain of the ballads have a peculiar and satisfying charm for me. To my mind, the incomparable Jungle Books must remain unfellowed permanently. I think it was worth the journey to India to qualify myself to read *Kim* understandingly and to realize how great a book it is. The deep and subtle and fascinating charm of India pervades no other book as it pervades *Kim*; *Kim* is pervaded by it as by an atmosphere. I read the book every year and in this way I go back to India without fatigue—the only foreign land I ever daydream about or deeply long to see again.

—1906

Elinor Glyn

Two or three weeks ago Elinor Glyn called on me one afternoon and we had a long talk, of a distinctly unusual character, in the library. It may be that by the time this chapter reaches print she may be less well known to the world than she is now, therefore I will insert here a word or two of information about her. She is English. She is an author. The newspapers say she is visiting America with the idea of finding just the right kind of a hero for the principal character in a romance which she is purposing to write. She has come to us upon the stormwind of a vast and sudden notoriety.

The source of this notoriety is a novel of hers called

Three Weeks. In this novel the hero is a fine and gifted and cultivated young English gentleman of good family, who imagines he has fallen in love with the ungifted, uninspired, commonplace daughter of the rector. He goes to the Continent on an outing, and there he happens upon a brilliant and beautiful young lady of exceedingly foreign extraction, with a deep mystery hanging over her. It transpires later that she is the childless wife of a king or kinglet, a coarse and unsympathetic animal whom she does not love.

She and the young Englishman fall in love with each other at sight. The hero's feeling for the rector's daughter was pale, not to say colorless, and it is promptly consumed and extinguished in the furnace fires of his passion for the mysterious stranger—passion is the right word, passion is what the pair of strangers feel for each other, what they recognize as real love—the only real love, the only love worthy to be called by that great name—whereas the feeling which the young man had for the rector's daughter is perceived to have been only a passing partiality.

The queenlet and the Englishman flit away privately to the mountains and take up sumptuous quarters in a remote and lonely house there—and then business begins. They recognize that they were highly and holily created for each other and that their passion is a sacred thing, that it is their master by divine right, and that its commands must be obeyed. They get to obeying them at once and they keep on obeying them and obeying them, to the reader's intense delight and disapproval, and the process of obeying them is described, several times, almost exhaustively, but not quite—some little rage of it being left to the reader's imagination, just at the end of each infraction, the place where his imagination is to take up and do the finish being indicated by stars.

The unstated argument of the book is that the laws of Nature are paramount and properly take precedence of the interfering and impertinent restrictions obtruded upon man's life by man's statutes.

Mme. Glyn called, as I have said, and she was a picture! Slender, young, faultlessly formed and incontestably beautiful—a blonde with blue eyes, the incomparable English complexion, and crowned with a glory of red hair of a very peculiar, most rare, and quite ravishing tint. She was clad in the choicest stuffs and in the most perfect taste. There she is, just a beautiful girl; yet she has a daughter fourteen years old. She isn't winning; she has no charm but the charm of beauty, and youth, and grace, and intelligence and vivacity; she *acts* charm, and does it well, exceedingly well in fact, but it does not convince, it doesn't stir the pulse, it doesn't go to the heart, it leaves the heart serene and unemotional. Her English hero would have prodigiously admired her; he would have loved to sit and look at her and hear her talk, but he would have been able to get away from that lonely house with his purity in good repair, if he wanted to.

I talked with her with daring frankness, frequently calling a spade a spade instead of coldly symbolizing it as a snow shovel; and on her side she was equally frank. It was one of the damnedest conversations I have ever had with a beautiful stranger of her sex, if I do say it myself that shouldn't. She wanted my opinion of her book and I furnished it. I said its literary workmanship was excellent, and that I quite agreed with her view that in the matter of the sexual relation man's statutory regulations of it were a distinct interference with a higher law, the law of Nature. I went further and said I couldn't call to mind a written law of any kind that had been promulgated in any age of the world in any statute book or any Bible for the regulation of man's conduct in *any* particular, from assassination all the way up to Sabbath-breaking, that wasn't a violation of the law of Nature, which I regarded as the highest of laws, the most peremptory and absolute of all laws—Nature's laws being in my belief plainly and simply the laws of God, since He instituted them, He and no other, and the said laws, by authority of this divine origin taking precedence of all the statutes of man. I said that her pair of indelicate lovers were obeying the law of their make and disposition; that therefore they were obeying the clearly enunciated law of God, and in His eyes must manifestly be blameless.

Of course what she wanted of me was support and defense—I knew that but I said I couldn't furnish it. I said we were the servants of convention; that we could not subsist, either in a savage or a civilized state, without conventions; that we must accept them and stand by them, even when we disapproved of them; that while the laws of Nature, that is to say the laws of God, plainly made every human being a law unto himself, we must steadfastly refuse to obey those laws, and we must as steadfastly stand by the conventions which ignore them, since the statutes furnish us peace, fairly good government, and stability, and therefore are better for us than the laws of God, which would soon plunge us into confusion and disorder and anarchy, if we should adopt them. I said her book was an assault upon certain old and well-established and wise conventions, and that it would not find many friends, and indeed would not deserve many.

She said I was very brave, the bravest person she had ever met (gross flattery which could have beguiled me when I was very very young), and she implored me to publish these views of mine, but I said, "No, such a thing is unthinkable." I said that if I, or any other wise, intelligent, and experienced person, should suddenly throw down the walls that protect and conceal his *real* opinions on almost any subject under the sun, it would at once be perceived that he had lost his intelligence and his wisdom and ought to be sent to the asylum. I said I had been revealing to her my private sentiments, *not* my public ones; that I, like all the other human beings, expose to the world only my trimmed and perfumed and carefully barbered public opinions and conceal carefully, cautiously, wisely, my private ones.

I explained that what I meant by that phrase "public opinions" was *published* opinions, opinions spread broadcast in print. I said I was in the common habit, in private conversations with friends, of revealing every private opinion I possessed relating to religion, politics, and men, but that I should never dream of *printing* one of them, because they are individually and collectively at war with almost everybody's public opinion, while at the same time they are in happy agreement with almost everybody's private opinion. As an instance, I asked her if she had ever encountered an intelligent person who privately believed in the Immaculate Conception—which of course she hadn't; and I also asked her if she had ever seen an intelligent person who was daring enough to publicly deny his belief in that fable and print the denial. Of course she hadn't encountered any such person.

I said I had a large cargo of most interesting and important private opinions about every great matter under the sun, but that they were not for print. I reminded her that we all break over the rule two or three times in our lives and fire a disagreeable and unpopular private opinion of ours into print, but we never do it when we can help it, we never do it except when the desire to do it is too strong for us and overrides and conquers our cold, calm, wise judgment. She mentioned several instances in which I had come out publicly in defense of unpopular causes, and she intimated that what I had been saying about myself was not perhaps in strict accordance with the facts; but I said they were merely illustrations of what I had just been saying, that when I publicly attacked the American missionaries in China and some other iniquitous persons and causes, I did not do it for any reason but just the one: that the inclination to do it was stronger than my diplomatic instincts, and I had to obey and take the consequences. But I said I was not moved to defend her book in public; that it was not a case where inclination was overpowering and unconquerable, and that therefore I could keep diplomatically still and should do it.

The lady was young enough, and inexperienced enough, to imagine that whenever a person has an unpleasant opinion in stock which could be of educational benefit to Tom, Dick, and Harry, it is his *duty* to come out in print with it and become its champion. I was not able to get that juvenile idea out of her head. I was not able to convince her that we never do any duty for the duty's sake but only for the mere personal satisfaction we get out of doing that duty. The fact is, she was brought up just like the rest of the world, with the ingrained and stupid superstition that there is such a thing as *duty for duty's sake*, and so I was obliged to let her abide in her darkness. She believed that when a man held a private unpleasant opinion of an educational sort, which would get him hanged if he published it, he ought to publish it anyway and was a coward if he didn't. Take it all around, it was a very pleasant conversation, and glaringly unprintable, particularly those considerable parts of it which I haven't had the courage to more than vaguely hint at in this account of our talk.

Some days afterward I met her again for a moment,

and she gave me the startling information that she had written down every word I had said, just as I had said it, without any softening and purifying modifications, and that it was "just splendid, just wonderful." She said she had sent it to her husband, in England. Privately I didn't think that that was a very good idea, and yet I believed it would interest him. She begged me to let her publish it and said it would do infinite good in the world, but I said it would damn me before my time and I didn't wish to be useful to the world on such expensive conditions.

—1908

Marie Corelli

I met Marie Corelli at a small dinner party in Germany fifteen years ago and took a dislike to her at once, a dislike which expanded and hardened with each successive dinner course until when we parted at last, the original mere dislike had grown into a very strong aversion. When I arrived in England, I found a letter from her awaiting me at Brown's Hotel. It was warm, affectionate, eloquent, persuasive; under its charm the aversion of fifteen years melted away and disappeared. It seemed to me that that aversion must have been falsely based; I thought I must certainly have been mistaken in the woman, and I felt a pang or two of remorse. I answered her letter at once—her love letter I may say—answered it with a love letter. Her home is in Shakespeare's Stratford. She at once wrote again, urging me in the most beguiling language to stop there and lunch with her when I should be on my way to London, on the 29th. It looked like an easy matter; the travel connected with it could not amount to much, I supposed, therefore I accepted by return mail.

I had now—not for the first time, nor the thousandth—trampled upon an old and wise and stern maxim of mine, to wit: "Supposing is good, but finding out is better." The supposing was finished, the letter was gone; it was now time to find out. Ashcroft [Clemens's secretary] examined the timetables and found that I would leave Oxford at eleven o'clock the 29th, leave Stratford at midafternoon, and not reach London until about half past six. That is to say, I would be seven and half hours in the air, so to speak, with no rest for the sole of my foot and a speech at the Lord Mayor's to follow! Necessarily I was aghast; I should probably arrive at the Lord Mayor's banquet in a hearse.

Ashcroft and I then began upon a hopeless task—to persuade a conscienceless fool to mercifully retire from a self-advertising scheme which was dear to her heart. She held her grip; anyone who knew her could have told us she would. She came to Oxford on the 29th to make sure of her prey. I begged her to let me off, I implored, I supplicated; I pleaded my white head and my seventy-two years and the likelihood that the long day in trains that would stop every three hundred yards and rest ten minutes would break me down and send me to the hospital. It had no effect. By God I might as well have pleaded with Shylock himself! She said she could not release me from my engagement; it would be quite impossible; and added, "Consider my side of the matter a little. I have invited Lady Lucy and two other ladies, and three gentlemen; to cancel the luncheon now would inflict upon them the greatest inconvenience; without doubt they have declined other invitations to accept this one; in my own case I have canceled three social engagements on account of this matter."

I said, "Which is the superior disaster: that your half-dozen guests be inconvenienced, or the Lord Mayor's three hundred? And if you have already canceled three engagements and thereby inconvenienced three sets of guests, canceling seems to come easy to you, and it looks as if you might add just one more to the list, in mercy to a suffering friend."

It hadn't the slightest effect; she was as hard as nails. I think there is no criminal in any jail with a heart so unmalleable, so unmeltable, so unfazeable, so flinty, so uncompromisingly hard as Marie Corelli's. I think one could hit it with a steel and draw a spark from it.

She is about fifty years old but has no gray hairs; she is fat and shapeless; she has a gross animal face; she dresses for sixteen, and awkwardly and unsuccessfully and pathetically imitates the innocent graces and witcheries of that dearest and sweetest of all ages; and so her exterior matches her interior and harmonizes with it, with the result—as I think—that she is the most offensive sham, inside and out, that misrepresents and satirizes the human race today. I would willingly say more about her but it would be futile to try; all the adjectives seem so poor and feeble and flabby, this morning.

So we went to Stratford by rail, with a car change or two, we not knowing that one could save time and fatigue by walking. She received us at Stratford station with her carriage and was going to drive us to Shakespeare's church, but I canceled that; she insisted but I said that day's program was already generous enough in fatigues without adding another. She said there would be a crowd at the church to welcome me and they would be greatly disappointed, but I was loaded to the chin with animosity and childishly eager to be as unpleasant as possible, so I held my ground, particularly as I was well acquainted with Marie by this time and foresaw that if I went to the church

I should find a trap arranged for a speech; my teeth were already loose from incessant speaking, and the very thought of adding a jabber at this time was a pain to me; besides, Marie, who never wastes an opportunity to advertise herself, would work the incident into the newspapers and I who could not waste any possible opportunity of disobliging her naturally made the best of this one.

She said she had been purchasing the house which the founder of Harvard College had once lived in and was going to present it to America—another advertisement. She wanted to stop at that dwelling and show me over it, and she said there would be a crowd there. I said I didn't want to see the damned house. I didn't say it in those words but in that vicious spirit, and she understood; even her horses understood and were shocked, for I saw them shudder. She pleaded and said we need not stop for more than a moment, but I knew the size of Marie's moments by now, when there was an advertisement to be had, and I declined. As we drove by I saw that the house and the sidewalk were full of people—which meant that Marie had arranged for another speech. However, we went by, bowing in response to the cheers, and presently reached Marie's house, a very attractive and commodious English home.

I said I was exceedingly tired and would like to go immediately to a bedchamber and stretch out and get some rest, if only for fifteen minutes. She was voluble with tender sympathy and said I should have my desire at once; but deftly steered me into the drawing-room and introduced me to her company. That being over, I begged leave to retire, but she wanted me to see her garden and said it would take only a moment. We examined her garden, I praising it and damning it in the one breath—

praising with the mouth and damning with the heart. Then she said there was another garden, and dragged me along to look at it. I was ready to drop with fatigue but I praised and damned as before, and hoped I was through now and might be suffered to die in peace; but she beguiled me to a grilled iron gate and pulled me through it into a stretch of waste ground where stood fifty pupils of a military school, with their master at their head—arrangement for another advertisement.

She asked me to make a little speech and said the boys were expecting it. I complied briefly, shook hands with the master and talked with him a moment, then—well then we got back to the house. I got a quarter of an hour's rest, then came down to the luncheon. Toward the end of it that implacable woman rose in her place, with a glass of champagne in her hand, and made a speech! With me for a text, of course. Another advertisement, you see—to be worked into the newspapers. When she had finished I said, "I thank you very much"—and sat still. This conduct of mine was compulsory, therefore not avoidable; if I had made a speech, courtesy and custom would have required me to construct it out of thanks and compliments, and there was not a rag of that kind of material lurking anywhere in my system.

We reached London at half past six in the evening in a pouring rain, and half an hour later I was in bed—in bed and tired to the very marrow; but the day was at an end, at any rate, and that was a comfort. This was the most hateful day my seventy-two years have ever known.

I have now exposed myself as being a person capable of entertaining and exhibiting a degraded and brutally ugly spirit, upon occasion, and in making this exposure I have done my duty by myself and by my reader—notwithstanding which I claim and maintain that in any other society than Marie Corelli's my spirit is the sweetest that has ever yet descended upon this planet from my ancestors, the angels.

I spoke at the Lord Mayor's banquet that night, and it was a botch.

Fenimore Cooper's Literary Offenses

> *The Pathfinder* and *The Deerslayer* stand at the head of Cooper's novels as artistic creations. There are others of his works which contain parts as perfect as are to be found in these, and scenes even more thrilling. Not one can be compared with either of them as a finished whole.
>
> The defects in both of these tales are comparatively slight. They were pure works of art.—*Prof. Lounsbury.*

> The five tales reveal an extraordinary fullness of invention. . . . One of the very greatest characters in fiction, Natty Bumppo. . . .
>
> The craft of the woodsman, the tricks of the trapper, all the delicate art of the forest, were familiar to Cooper from his youth up.—*Prof. Brander Matthews.*

> Cooper is the greatest artist in the domain of romantic fiction yet produced by America.—*Wilkie Collins.*

It seems to me that it was far from right for the Professor of English Literature in Yale, the Professor of English Literature in Columbia, and Wilkie Collins to deliver opinions on Cooper's literature without having read some of it. It would have been much more decorous to keep silent and let persons talk who have read Cooper.

Cooper's art has some defects. In one place in *Deerslayer,* and in the restricted space of two-thirds of a page, Cooper has scored 114 offenses against literary art out of a possible 115. It breaks the record.

There are nineteen rules governing literary art in the domain of romantic fiction—some say twenty-two. In *Deerslayer* Cooper violated eighteen of them. These eighteen require:

1. That a tale shall accomplish something and arrive somewhere. But the *Deerslayer* tale accomplishes nothing and arrives in the air.

2. They require that the episodes of a tale shall be necessary parts of the tale and shall help to develop it. But as the *Deerslayer* tale is not a tale and accomplishes nothing and arrives nowhere, the episodes have no rightful place in the work, since there was nothing for them to develop.

3. They require that the personages in a tale shall be alive, except in the case of corpses, and that always the reader shall be able to tell the corpses from the others. But this detail has often been overlooked in the *Deerslayer* tale.

4. They require that the personages in a tale, both dead and alive, shall exhibit a sufficient excuse for being there. But this detail also has been overlooked in the *Deerslayer* tale.

5. They require that when the personages of a tale deal in conversation, the talk shall sound like human talk, and be talk such as human beings would be likely to talk in the given circumstances, and have a discoverable meaning, also a discoverable purpose and show of relevancy, and remain in the neighborhood of the subject in hand, and be interesting to the reader, and help out the tale, and stop when the people cannot think of anything more to say. But this requirement has been ignored from the beginning of the *Deerslayer* tale to the end of it.

6. They require that when the author describes the character of a personage in his tale, the conduct and conversation of that personage shall justify said description.

But this law gets little or no attention in the *Deerslayer* tale, as Natty Bumppo's case will amply prove.

7. They require that when a personage talks like an illustrated, gilt-edged, tree-calf, hand-tooled, seven-dollar Friendship's Offering in the beginning of a paragraph, he shall not talk like a negro minstrel in the end of it. But this rule is flung down and danced upon in the *Deerslayer* tale.

8. They require that crass stupidities shall not be played upon the reader as "the craft of the woodsman, the delicate art of the forest," by either the author or the people in the tale. But this rule is persistently violated in the *Deerslayer* tale.

9. They require that the personages of a tale shall confine themselves to possibilities and let miracles alone; or, if they venture a miracle, the author must so plausibly set it forth as to make it look possible and reasonable. But these rules are not respected in the *Deerslayer* tale.

10. They require that the author shall make the reader feel a deep interest in the personages of his tale and in their fate, and that he shall make the reader love the good people in the tale and hate the bad ones. But the reader of the *Deerslayer* tale dislikes the good people in it, is indifferent to the others, and wishes they would all get drowned together.

11. They require that the characters in a tale shall be so clearly defined that the reader can tell beforehand what each will do in a given emergency. But in the *Deerslayer* tale this rule is vacated.

In addition to these large rules there are some little ones. These require that the author shall:

12. *Say* what he is proposing to say, not merely come near it.

13. Use the right word, not its second cousin.

14. Eschew surplusage.

15. Not omit necessary details.
16. Avoid slovenliness of form.
17. Use good grammar.
18. Employ a simple and straightforward style.

Even these seven are coldly and persistently violated in the *Deerslayer* tale.

Cooper's gift in the way of invention was not a rich endowment but such as it was he liked to work it, he was pleased with the effects, and indeed he did some quite sweet things with it. In his little box of stage-properties he kept six or eight cunning devices, tricks, artifices for his savages and woodsmen to deceive and circumvent each other with, and he was never so happy as when he was working these innocent things and seeing them go. A favorite one was to make a moccasined person tread in the tracks of the moccasined enemy, and thus hide his own trail. Cooper wore out barrels and barrels of moccasins in working that trick. Another stage-property that he pulled out of his box pretty frequently was his broken twig. He prized his broken twig above all the rest of his effects, and worked it the hardest. It is a restful chapter in any book of his when somebody doesn't step on a dry twig and alarm all the reds and whites for two hundred yards around. Every time a Cooper person is in peril and absolute silence is worth four dollars a minute, he is sure to step on a dry twig. There may be a hundred handier things to step on but that wouldn't satisfy Cooper. Cooper requires him to turn out and find a dry twig, and if he can't do it, go and borrow one. In fact, the Leatherstocking Series ought to have been called the Broken Twig Series.

I am sorry there is not room to put in a few dozen instances of the delicate art of the forest, as practised by Natty Bumppo and some of the other Cooperian experts. Perhaps we may venture two or three samples. Cooper was a sailor, a naval officer; yet he gravely tells us how a vessel, driving toward a lee shore in a gale, is steered for a particular spot by her skipper because he knows of an *undertow* there which will hold her back against the gale and save her. For just pure woodcraft, or sailorcraft, or whatever it is, isn't that neat? For several years Cooper was daily in the society of artillery and he ought to have noticed that when a cannon-ball strikes the ground it either buries itself or skips a hundred feet or so, skips again a hundred feet or so, and so on till finally it gets tired and rolls. Now in one place he loses some "females"—as he always calls women—in the edge of a wood near a plain at night in a fog, on purpose to give Bumppo a chance to show off the delicate art of the forest before the reader. These mislaid people are hunting for a fort. They hear a cannon-blast, and a cannon-ball presently comes rolling into the wood and stops at their feet. To the females this suggests nothing. The case is very different with the admirable Bumppo. I wish I may never know peace again if he doesn't strike out promptly and *follow the track* of that cannon-ball across the plain through the dense fog and find the fort. Isn't it a daisy? If Cooper had any real knowledge of Nature's ways of doing things, he had a most delicate art in concealing the fact. For instance: one of his acute Indian experts, Chingachgook (pronounced Chicago, I think), has lost the trail of a person he is tracking through the forest. Apparently that trail is hopelessly lost. Neither you nor I could ever have guessed out the way to find it. It was very different with Chicago. Chicago was not stumped for long. He turned a running stream out of its course and there, in the slush in its old bed, were that person's moccasin tracks. The current did not wash them away, as it would have done in all other like cases—no, even the eternal laws of Nature have to vacate when Cooper wants to put up a delicate job of woodcraft on the reader.

We must be a little wary when Brander Matthews tells us that Cooper's books "reveal an extraordinary fullness of invention." As a rule, I am quite willing to accept Brander Matthews's literary judgments and applaud his lucid and graceful phrasing of them, but that particular statement needs to be taken with a few tons of salt. Bless your heart, Cooper hadn't any more invention than a horse, and I don't mean a high-class horse, either, I mean a clothes-horse. It would be very difficult to find a really clever "situation" in Cooper's books, and still more difficult to find one of any kind which he has failed to render absurd by his handling of it. Look at the episode of "the caves"; and at the celebrated scuffle between Maqua and those others on the table-land a few days later; and at Hurry Harry's queer water-transit from the castle to the ark; and at Deerslayer's half-hour with his first corpse; and at the quarrel between Hurry Harry and *Deerslayer* later; and at—But choose for yourself, you can't go amiss.

If Cooper had been an observer his inventive faculty would have worked better: not more interestingly but more rationally, more plausibly. Cooper's proudest creations in the way of "situations" suffer noticeably from the absence of the observer's protecting gift. Cooper's eye was splendidly inaccurate. Cooper seldom saw anything correctly. He saw nearly all things as through a glass eye, darkly. Of course a man who cannot see the commonest little every-day matters accurately is working at a disadvantage when he is constructing a "situation." In the *Deerslayer* tale Cooper has a stream which is fifty feet wide where it flows out of a lake; it presently narrows to twenty as it meanders along for no given reason, and yet when a stream acts like that it ought to be required to explain itself. Fourteen pages later the width of the brook's outlet from the lake has suddenly shrunk thirty feet and become "the narrowest part of the stream." This shrinkage is not accounted for. The stream has bends in it, a sure indication that it has alluvial banks and cuts them, yet these bends are only thirty and fifty feet long. If Cooper had been a nice and punctilious observer he would have noticed that the bends were oftener nine hundred feet long than short of it.

Cooper made the exit of that stream fifty feet wide in the first place for no particular reason; in the second place, he narrowed it to less than twenty to accommodate some Indians. He bends a "sapling" to the form of an arch over this narrow passage and conceals six Indians in its foliage. They are "laying" for a settler's scow or ark which is coming up the stream on its way to the lake; it is being hauled against the stiff current by a rope whose stationary end is anchored in the lake; its rate of progress cannot be more than a mile an hour. Cooper describes the ark, but pretty obscurely. In the matter of dimensions "it was little more than a modern canal-boat." Let us guess, then, that it was about one hundred and forty feet long. It was of "greater breadth than common." Let us guess, then, that it was about sixteen feet wide. This leviathan had been prowling down bends which were but a third as long as itself and scraping between banks where it had only two feet of space to spare on each side. We cannot too much admire this miracle. A low-roofed log dwelling occupies "two-thirds of the ark's length"—a dwelling ninety feet long and sixteen feet wide, let us say, a kind of vestibule train. The dwelling has two rooms, each forty-five feet long and sixteen feet wide, let us guess. One of them is the bedroom of the Hutter girls, Judith and Hetty; the other is the parlor in the daytime, at night it is papa's bed-chamber. The ark is arriving at the stream's exit now, whose width has been reduced to less than twenty feet to accommodate the Indians—say to eighteen. There is a foot to spare on each side of the boat. Did the Indians notice that there was going to be a tight squeeze there? Did they notice that they could make money by climbing down out of that arched sapling and just stepping aboard when the ark scraped by? No, other Indians would have noticed these things but Cooper's Indians never notice anything. Cooper thinks they are marvelous creatures for noticing but he was almost always in error about his Indians. There was seldom a sane one among them.

The ark is one hundred and forty feet long; the dwelling is ninety feet long. The idea of the Indians is to drop softly and secretly from the arched sapling to the dwelling as the ark creeps along under it at the rate of a mile an hour, and butcher the family. It will take the ark a minute and a half to pass under. It will take the ninety-foot dwelling a minute to pass under. Now, then, what did the six Indians do? It would take you thirty years to guess and even then you would have to give up, I believe. Therefore, I will tell you what the Indians did. Their chief, a person of quite extraordinary intellect for a Cooper Indian, warily watched the canal-boat as it squeezed along under him and when he had got his calculations fined down to exactly the right shade, as he judged, he let go and dropped. And *missed the house*! That is actually what he did. He missed the house and landed in the stern of the scow. It was not much of a fall, yet it knocked him silly. He lay there unconscious. If the house had been ninety-seven feet long he would have made the trip. The fault was Cooper's, not his. The error lay in the construction of the house. Cooper was no architect.

There still remained in the roost five Indians. The boat has passed under and is now out of their reach. Let me explain what the five did—you would not be able to reason it out for yourself. No. 1 jumped for the boat but fell in the water astern of it. Then No. 2 jumped for the boat but fell in the water still farther astern of it. Then No. 3 jumped for the boat and fell a good way astern of it. Then No. 4 jumped for the boat and fell in the water *away* astern. Then even No. 5 made a jump for the boat—for he was a Cooper Indian. In the matter of intellect, the difference between a Cooper Indian and the Indian that stands in front of the cigar shop is not spacious. The scow episode is really a sublime burst of invention but it does not thrill, because the inaccuracy of the details throws a sort of air of fictitiousness and general improbability over it. This comes of Cooper's inadequacy as an observer.

The reader will find some samples of Cooper's high talent for inaccurate observation in the account of the shooting-match in *The Pathfinder*.

> A common wrought nail was driven lightly into the target, its head having been first touched with paint.

The color of the paint is not stated—an important omission, but Cooper deals freely in important omissions. No, after all, it was not an important omission, for this nail-head is a *hundred yards from* the marksmen and could not be seen by them at that distance, no matter what its color might be. How far can the best eyes see a common house-fly? A hundred yards? It is quite impossible. Very well, eyes that cannot see a house-fly that is a hundred yards away cannot see an ordinary nail-head at that distance, for the size of the two objects is the same. It takes a keen eye to see a fly or a nail-head at fifty yards—one hundred and fifty feet. Can the reader do it?

The nail was lightly driven, its head painted, and game

called. Then the Cooper miracles began. The bullet of the first marksman chipped an edge of the nailhead; the next man's bullet drove the nail a little way into the target—and removed all the paint. Haven't the miracles gone far enough now? Not to suit Cooper, for the purpose of this whole scheme is to show off his prodigy, Deerslayer-Hawkeye-Long-Rifle-Leatherstocking-Pathfinder-Bumppo before the ladies.

> "Be all ready to clench it, boys!" cried out Pathfinder, stepping into his friend's tracks the instant they were vacant. "Never mind a new nail; I can see that, though the paint is gone, and what I can see I can hit at a hundred yards, though it were only a mosquito's eye. Be ready to clench!"
>
> The rifle cracked, the bullet sped its way, and the head of the nail was buried in the wood, covered by the piece of flattened lead.

There, you see, is a man who could hunt flies with a rifle, and command a ducal salary in a Wild West show today if we had him back with us.

The recorded feat is certainly surprising just as it stands, but it is not surprising enough for Cooper. Cooper adds a touch. He has made Pathfinder do this miracle with another man's rifle; and not only that, but Pathfinder did not have even the advantage of loading it himself. He had everything against him, and yet he made that impossible shot, and not only made it but did it with absolute confidence, saying, "Be ready to clench." Now a person like that would have undertaken the same feat with a brickbat, and with Cooper to help he would have achieved it, too.

Pathfinder showed off handsomely that day before the ladies. His very first feat was a thing which no Wild West show can touch. He was standing with the group of marksmen, observing—a hundred yards from the target, mind; one Jasper raised his rifle and drove the center of the bull's-eye. Then the Quartermaster fired. The target exhibited no result this time. There was a laugh. "It's a dead miss," said Major Lundie. Pathfinder waited an impressive moment or two, then said in that calm, indifferent, know-it-all way of his, "No, Major, he has covered Jasper's bullet, as will be seen if anyone will take the trouble to examine the target.

Wasn't it remarkable! How *could* he see that little pellet fly through the air and enter that distant bullet-hole? Yet that is what he did, for nothing is impossible to a Cooper person. Did any of those people have any deep-seated doubts about this thing? No; for that would imply sanity and these were all Cooper people.

> The respect for Pathfinder's skill and for *his quickness and accuracy of sight* [the italics are mine] was so profound and general, that the instant he made this declaration the spectators began to distrust their own opinions, and a dozen rushed to the target in order to ascertain the fact. There, sure enough, it was found that the Quartermaster's bullet had gone through the hole made by Jasper's, and that, too, so accurately as to require a minute examination to be certain of the circumstance, which, however, was soon clearly established by discovering one bullet over the other in the stump against which the target was placed.

They made a "minute" examination; but never mind, how could they know that there were two bullets in that hole without digging the latest one out? for neither probe nor eyesight could prove the presence of any more than one bullet. Did they dig? No; as we shall see. It is the Pathfinder's turn now; he steps out before the ladies, takes aim, and fires.

But, alas! here is a disappointment, an incredible, an

unimaginable disappointment—for the target's aspect is unchanged; there is nothing there but that same old bullet-hole!

> "If one dared to hint at such a thing," cried Major Duncan, "I should say that the Pathfinder has also missed the target!"

As nobody had missed it yet, the "also" was not necessary, but never mind about that for the Pathfinder is going to speak.

> "No, no, Major," said he, confidently, "that *would* be a risky declaration. I didn't load the piece, and can't say what was in it; but if it was lead, you will find the bullet driving down those of the Quartermaster and Jasper, else is not my name Pathfinder."
>
> A shout from the target announced the truth of this assertion.

Is the miracle sufficient as it stands? Not for Cooper. The Pathfinder speaks again, as he "now slowly advances toward the stage occupied by the females":

> "That's not all, boys, that's not all; if you find the target touched at all, I'll own to a miss. The Quartermaster cut the wood, but you'll find no wood cut by that last messenger."

The miracle is at last complete. He knew—doubtless *saw*—at the distance of a hundred yards—that his bullet had passed into the hole *without fraying the edges.* There were now three bullets in that one hole, three bullets embedded processionally in the body of the stump back of the target. Everybody knew this, somehow or other, and yet nobody had dug any of them out to make sure. Cooper is not a close observer but he is interesting. He is certainly always that, no matter what happens. And he is more interesting when he is not noticing what he is about than when he is. This is a considerable merit.

The conversations in the Cooper books have a curious sound in our modern ears. To believe that such talk really ever came out of people's mouths would be to believe that there was a time when time was of no value to a person who thought he had something to say, when it was the custom to spread a two-minute remark out to ten, when a man's mouth was a rolling-mill and busied itself all day long in turning four-foot pigs of thought into thirty-foot bars of conversational railroad iron by attenuation, when subjects were seldom faithfully stuck to but the talk wandered all around and arrived nowhere, when conversations consisted mainly of irrelevancies with here and there a relevancy, a relevancy with an embarrassed look, as not being able to explain how it got there.

Cooper was certainly not a master in the construction of dialogue. Inaccurate observation defeated him here as it defeated him in so many other enterprises of his. He even failed to notice that the man who talks corrupt English six days in the week must and will talk it on the seventh, and can't help himself. In the *Deerslayer* story he lets *Deerslayer* talk the showiest kind of book-talk sometimes, and at other times the basest of base dialects. For instance, when some one asks him if he has a sweetheart, and if so where she abides, this is his majestic answer:

> "She's in the forest—hanging from the boughs of the trees, in a soft rain—in the dew on the open grass—the clouds that float about in the blue heavens—the birds that sing in the woods—the sweet springs where I slake my thirst—and in all the other glorious gifts that come from God's Providence!"

And he preceded that, a little before, with this:

> "It consarns me as all things that touches a fri'nd consarns a fri'nd."

And this is another of his remarks:

> "If I was Injin born, now, I might tell of this, or carry in the scalp and boast of the expl'ite afore the whole tribe; or if my inimy had only been a bear"—[and so on].

We cannot imagine such a thing as a veteran Scotch Commander-in-Chief comporting himself in the field like a windy melodramatic actor, but Cooper could. On one occasion Alice and Cora were being chased by the French through a fog in the neighborhood of their father's fort:

> *"Point de quartier aux coquins!"* cried an eager pursuer, who seemed to direct the operations of the enemy.
>
> "Stand firm and be ready, my gallant 60ths!" suddenly exclaimed a voice above them; "wait to see the enemy; fire low, and sweep the glacis."
>
> "Father! father," exclaimed a piercing cry from out the mist; "it is I! Alice! thy own Elsie! spare, O! save your daughters!"
>
> "Hold!" shouted the former speaker, in the awful tones of parental agony, the sound reaching even to the woods, and rolling back in solemn echo. " 'Tis she! God has restored me my children! Throw open the sally-port; to the field, 60ths, to the field! pull not a trigger, lest ye kill my lambs! Drive off these dogs of France with your steel!"

Cooper's word-sense was singularly dull. When a person has a poor ear for music he will flat and sharp right along without knowing it. He keeps near the tune, but it is *not* the tune. When a person has a poor ear for words, the result is a literary flatting and sharping; you perceive what he is intending to say but you also perceive that he doesn't *say* it. This is Cooper. He was not a word-musician. His ear was satisfied with the *approximate* word. I will furnish some circumstantial evidence in support of this charge. My instances are gathered from half a dozen pages of the tale called *Deerslayer*. He uses "verbal" for "oral"; "precision" for "facility"; "phenomena" for "marvels"; "necessary" for "predetermined"; "unsophisticated" for "primitive"; "preparation" for "expectancy"; "rebuked" for "subdued"; "dependent on" for "resulting from"; "fact" for "condition"; "fact" for "conjecture"; "precaution" for "caution"; "explain" for "determine"; "mortified" for "disappointed"; "meretricious" for "factitious"; "materially" for "considerably"; "decreasing" for "deepening"; "increasing" for "disappearing"; "embedded" for "inclosed"; "treacherous" for "hostile"; "stood" for "stooped"; "softened" for "replaced"; "rejoined" for "remarked"; "situation" for "condition"; "different" for "differing"; "insensible" for "unsentient"; "brevity" for "celerity"; "distrusted" for "suspicious"; "mental imbecility" for "imbecility"; "eyes" for "sight"; "counteracting" for "opposing"; "funeral obsequies" for "obsequies."

There have been daring people in the world who claimed that Cooper could write English but they are all dead now—all dead but Lounsbury. I don't remember that Lounsbury makes the claim in so many words, still he makes it for he says that *Deerslayer* is a "pure work of art." Pure, in that connection, means faultless—faultless in all details—and language is a detail. If Mr. Lounsbury had only compared Cooper's English with the English which he writes himself—but it is plain that he didn't, and so it is likely that he imagines until this day that Cooper's is as clean and compact as his own. Now I feel sure, deep down in my heart, that Cooper wrote about the poorest English that exists in our language and that the English of *Deerslayer* is the very worst that even Cooper ever wrote.

I may be mistaken, but it does seem to me that *Deerslayer* is not a work of art in any sense; it does seem to me that it is destitute of every detail that goes to the making of a work of art; in truth, it seems to me that *Deerslayer* is just simply a literary *delirium tremens.*

A work of art? It has no invention; it has no order, system, sequence, or result; it has no lifelikeness, no thrill, no stir, no seeming of reality; its characters are confusedly drawn and by their acts and words they prove that they are not the sort of people the author claims that they are; its humor is pathetic; its pathos is funny; its conversations are—oh! indescribable; its love-scenes odious; its English a crime against the language.

Counting these out, what is left is Art. I think we must all admit that.

Bret Harte

How wonderful are the ways of Providence! But I will take that up later.

About forty years ago—I was a reporter on the *Morning Call* of San Francisco. I was more than that—I was *the* reporter. There was no other. There was enough work for one and a little over, but not enough for two—according to Mr. Barnes's idea, and he was the proprietor and therefore better situated to know about it than other people.

In those ancient times the counting room of the *Morning Call* was on the ground floor; the office of the Superintendent of the United States Mint was on the next floor above, with Bret Harte as private secretary of the

Superintendent. The quarters of the editorial staff and the reporter were on the third floor, and the composing room on the fourth and final floor. I spent a good deal of time with Bret Harte in his office after Smiggy McGlural came, but not before that. Harte was doing a good deal of writing for the *Californian*—contributing "Condensed Novels" and sketches to it and also acting as editor, I think. I was a contributor. So was Charles H. Webb; also Prentiss Mulford; also a young lawyer named Hastings, who gave promise of distinguishing himself in literature some day. Charles Warren Stoddard was a contributor. Ambrose Bierce, who is still writing acceptably for the magazines today, was then employed on some paper in San Francisco—*The Golden Era*, perhaps. We had very good times together—very social and pleasant times. But that was after Smiggy McGlural came to my assistance; there was no leisure before that. Smiggy was a great advantage to me—during thirty days. Then he turned into a disaster.

It was Mr. Swain, Superintendent of the Mint, who discovered Bret Harte. Harte had arrived in California in the fifties, twenty-three or twenty-four years old, and had wandered up into the surface diggings of the camp at Yreka, a place which had acquired its curious name—when in its first days it much needed a name—through an accident. There was a bakeshop with a canvas sign which had not yet been put up but had been painted and stretched to dry in such a way that the word BAKERY, all but the B, showed through and was reversed. A stranger read it wrong end first, YREKA, and supposed that that was the name of the camp. The campers were satisfied with it and adopted it.

Harte taught school in that camp several months. He also edited the weekly rag which was doing duty as a newspaper. He spent a little time also in the pocket-mining camp of Jackass Gulch (where I tarried, some years later, during three months). It was at Yreka and Jackass Gulch that Harte learned to accurately observe and put with photographic exactness on paper the woodland scenery of California and the general country aspects—the stagecoach, its driver and its passengers, and the clothing and general style of the surface miner, the gambler, and their women; and it was also in these places that he learned, without the trouble of observing, all that he didn't know about mining, and how to make it read as if an expert were behind the pen. It was in those places that he also learned how to fascinate Europe and America with the quaint dialect of the miner—a dialect which no man in heaven or earth had ever used until Harte invented it. With Harte it died, but it was no loss. By and by he came to San Francisco. He was a compositor by trade, and got work in *The Golden Era* office at ten dollars a week.

Harte was paid for setting type only but he lightened his labors and entertained himself by contributing literature to the paper, uninvited. The editor and proprietor, Joe Lawrence, never saw Harte's manuscripts, because there weren't any. Harte spun his literature out of his head while at work at the case, and set it up as he spun. *The Golden Era* was ostensibly and ostentatiously a literary paper, but its literature was pretty feeble and sloppy and only exhibited the literary forms, without really being literature. Mr. Swain, the Superintendent of the Mint, noticed a new note in the *Golden Era* orchestra—a new and fresh and spirited note that rose above that orchestra's mumbling confusion and was recognizable as music. He asked Joe Lawrence who the performer was, and Lawrence told him. It seemed to Mr. Swain a shame that Harte should be wasting himself in such a place and on such a pittance so he took him away, made him his private secretary, on a good salary, with little or nothing to do, and told him to follow his own bent and develop his talent. Harte was willing and the development began.

Bret Harte was one of the pleasantest men I have ever known. He was also one of the unpleasantest men I have ever known. He was showy, meretricious, insincere; and he constantly advertised these qualities in his dress. He was distinctly pretty, in spite of the fact that his face was badly pitted with smallpox. In the days when he could afford it—and in the days when he couldn't—his clothes always exceeded the fashion by a shade or two. He was always conspicuously a little more intensely fashionable than the fashionablest of the rest of the community. He had good taste in clothes. With all his conspicuousness there was never anything really loud nor offensive about them. They always had a single smart little accent, effectively located and that accent would have distinguished Harte from any other of the ultra-fashionables. Oftenest it was his necktie. Always it was a single color, and intense. Most frequently, perhaps, it was crimson—a flash of flame under his chin; or it was indigo blue and as hot and vivid as if one of those splendid and luminous Brazilian butterflies had lighted there. Harte's dainty self-complacencies extended to his carriage and gait. His carriage was graceful and easy, his gait was of the mincing sort, but was the right gait for him, for an unaffected one would not have harmonized with the rest of the man and the clothes.

He hadn't a sincere fiber in him. I think he was incapable of emotion, for I think he had nothing to feel with, I think his heart was merely a pump and had no other function. I am almost moved to say I *know* it had no other function. I knew him intimately in the days when he was private secretary on the second floor and I a fading and perishing reporter on the third, with Smiggy McGlural looming doomfully in the near distance. I knew him intimately when he came east five years later, in 1870, to take the editorship of the proposed *Lakeside Magazine*, in Chicago, and crossed the continent through such a prodigious blaze of national interest and excitement that one might have supposed he was the Viceroy of India on a progress, or Halley's comet come again after seventy-five years of lamented absence.

I knew him pretty intimately thenceforth until he crossed the ocean to be consul, first at Crefeldt in Germany and afterwards in Glasgow. He never returned to America. When he died, in London, he had been absent from America and from his wife and daughters twenty-six years.

This is the very Bret Harte whose pathetics, imitated from Dickens, used to be a godsend to the farmers of two hemispheres on account of the freshets of tears they compelled. He said to me once with a cynical chuckle that he thought he had mastered the art of pumping up the tear of sensibility. The idea conveyed was that the tear of sensibility was oil, and that by luck he had struck it.

It is a pity that we cannot escape from life when we are young. When Bret Harte started east in his newborn glory thirty-six years ago, with the eyes of the world upon him, he had lived all of his life that was worth living. He had lived all of his life that was to be respectworthy. He had lived all of his life that was to be worthy of his *own* respect. He was entering upon a miserable career of poverty, debt, humiliation, shame, disgrace, bitterness, and a world-wide fame which must have often been odious to him, since it made his poverty and the shabbiness of his character conspicuous beyond the power of any art to mercifully hide them.

There was a happy Bret Harte, a connected Bret Harte,

an ambitious Bret Harte, a hopeful Bret Harte, a bright, cheerful, easy-laughing Bret Harte, a Bret Harte to whom it was a bubbling and effervescent joy to be alive. That Bret Harte died in San Francisco. It was the corpse of that Bret Harte that swept in splendor across the continent; that refused to go to the Chicago banquet given in his honor because there had been a breach of etiquette—a carriage had not been sent for it; that resumed its eastward journey behind the grand scheme of the *Lakeside Monthly* in sorrowful collapse; that undertook to give all the product of its brain for one year to the *Atlantic Monthly* for ten thousand dollars—a stupendous sum in those days—furnished nothing worth speaking of for the great pay, but collected and spent the money before the year was out, and then began a dismal and harassing death-in-life of borrowing from men and living on women which was to cease only at the grave.

—1906

In these days things are happening which bring Bret Harte to my mind again; they rake up memories of him which carry me back thirty and forty years. He had a curious adventure once, when he was a young chap new to the Pacific Coast and floating around seeking bread and butter. He told me some of his experiences of that early day. For a while he taught a school in the lively gold-mining camp of Yreka, and at the same time he added a trifle to his income by editing the little weekly local journal for the pair of journeymen typesetters who owned it.

His duties as editor required him to read proof. Once a galley slip was laid before him which consisted of one of those old-time obituaries which were so dismally popular all over the United States when we were still a soft-hearted and sentimental people. There was half a column of the obituary and it was built upon the regulation plan; that is to say, it was made up of superlatives—superlatives wherewith the writer tried to praise Mrs. Thompson, the deceased, to the summit of her merit, the result being a flowery, overheated, and most extravagant eulogy, and closing with that remark which was never missing from the regulation obituary: "Our loss is her eternal gain."

In the proof Harte found this observation: "Even in Yreka her chastity was conspicuous." Of course that word was a misprint for "charity," but Harte didn't think of that; he knew a printer's mistake had been made and he also knew that a reference to the manuscript would determine what it was; therefore he followed proofreader custom and with his pen indicated in the usual way that the manuscript must be examined. It was a simple matter and took only a moment of his time; he drew a black line under the word chastity, and in the margin he placed a question mark enclosed in parentheses. It was a brief way of saying, "There is something the matter with this word; examine the manuscript and make the necessary correction." But there is another proofreader law which he overlooked. That law says that when a word is not emphatic enough you must draw a line under it, and this will require the printer to reinforce it by putting it in italics.

When Harte took up the paper in the morning and looked at that obituary he took only one glance; then he levied on a mule that was not being watched and cantered out of town, knowing well that in a very little while there was going to be a visit from the widower, with his gun. In the obituary the derelict observation now stood in this form: "Even in Yreka her *chastity* was conspicuous (?)"—a form which turned the thing into a ghastly and ill-timed sarcasm!

I am reminded, in a wide roundabout way, of another

of Harte's adventures, by a remark in a letter lately received from Tom Fitch, whom Joe Goodman crippled in the duel—for Tom Fitch is still alive, although inhabiting Arizona. After wandering for years and years all about the planet, Fitch has gone back to his early loves, the sand, the sagebrush, and the jackass rabbit; and these things, and the old-time ways of the natives, have refreshed his spirit and restored to him his lost youth. Those friendly people slap him on the shoulder and call him—well, never mind what they call him; it might offend your ears, but it does Fitch's heart good. He knows its deep meanings; he recognizes the affection that is back of it, and so it is music to his spirit, and he is grateful.

When "The Luck of Roaring Camp" burst upon the world Harte became instantly famous; his name and his praises were upon every lip. One day he had occasion to go to Sacramento. When he went ashore there he forgot to secure a berth for the return trip. When he came down to the landing, in the later afternoon, he realized that he had made a calamitous blunder; apparently all Sacramento was proposing to go down to San Francisco; there was a queue of men which stretched from the purser's office down the gangplank, across the levee, and up the street out of sight.

Harte had one hope: inasmuch as in theaters, operas, steamboats, and steamships, half a dozen choice places are always reserved to be conferred upon belated clients of distinction, perhaps his name might procure for him one of those reserved places, if he could smuggle his card to the purser; so he edged his way along the queue and at last stood shoulder to shoulder with a vast and rugged miner from the mountains, who had his revolvers in his belt, whose great slouch hat overshadowed the whiskered face of a buccaneer, and whose raiment was splashed with clay from his chin down to his boot tops. The queue was drifting slowly by the purser's wicket, and each member of it was hearing, in his turn, the fatal words: "No berths left; not even floor space." The purser was just saying it to the truculent big miner when Harte passed his card in. The purser exclaimed, passing a key, "Ah, Mr. Bret Harte, glad to see you sir! Take the whole stateroom, sir."

The bedless miner cast a scowl upon Harte which shed a twilight gloom over the whole region and frightened that author to such a degree that his key and its wooden tag rattled in his quaking hand; then he disappeared from the miner's view and sought seclusion and safety behind the lifeboats and such things on the hurricane deck. But nevertheless the thing happened which he was expecting—the miner soon appeared up there and went peering around; whenever he approached dangerously near, Harte shifted his shelter and hid behind a new one. This went on without unhappy accident for half an hour, but at last failure came: Harte made a miscalculation; he crept cautiously out from behind a lifeboat and came face to face with the miner! He felt that it was an awful situation, a fatal situation but it was not worth while to try to escape, so he stood still and waited for his doom. The miner said, sternly, "Are you Bret Harte?"

Harte confessed it in a feeble voice.

"Did you write that 'Luck of Roaring Camp'?"

Harte confessed again.

"Sure?"

"Yes"—in a whisper.

The miner burst out, fervently and affectionately, "*Son* of a ——! Put it there!" and he gripped Harte's hand in his mighty talons and mashed it.

Tom Fitch knows that welcome phrase, and the love and admiration that purge it of its earthiness and make it divine.

In the early days I liked Bret Harte, and so did the others, but by and by I got over it; so also did the others. He couldn't keep a friend permanently. He was bad, distinctly bad; he had no feeling, and he had no conscience. His wife was all that a good woman, a good wife, a good mother, and a good friend, can be; but when he went to Europe as consul he left her and his little children behind, and never came back again from that time until his death, twenty-six years later.

He was an incorrigible borrower of money; he borrowed from all his friends; if he ever repaid a loan the incident failed to pass into history. He was always ready to give his note but the matter ended there. We sailed for Europe on the 10th of April, 1878, and on the preceding night there was a banquet to Bayard Taylor, who was going out in the same ship as our minister to Germany. At that dinner I met a gentleman whose society I found delightful, and we became very friendly and communicative. He fell to talking about Bret Harte, and it soon appeared that he had a grievance against him. He had so admired Harte's writings that he had greatly desired to know Harte himself.

The acquaintanceship was achieved and the borrowing began. The man was rich and he lent gladly. Harte always gave his note, and of his own motion, for it was not required of him. Harte had then been in the East about eight years, and these borrowings had been going on during several of those years; in the aggregate they amounted to about three thousand dollars. The man told me that Harte's notes were a distress to him because he supposed that they were a distress to Harte.

Then he had what he thought was a happy idea: he compacted the notes into a bale and sent them to Harte on the 24th of December '77 as a Christmas present; and with them he sent a note begging Harte to allow him this privilege because of the warm and kind and brotherly feeling which prompted it. Per next day's mail Harte fired the bale back at him, accompanying it with a letter which was all afire with insulted dignity, and which formally and by irrevocable edict permanently annulled the existing friendship. But there was nothing in it about paying the notes sometime or other.

When Harte made his spectacular progress across the continent in 1870, he took up his residence at Newport, Rhode Island, that breeding place—that stud farm, so to speak—of aristocracy; aristocracy of the American type; that auction mart where the English nobilities come to trade hereditary titles for American girls and cash. Within a twelvemonth he had spent his ten thousand dollars and he shortly thereafter left Newport, in debt to the butcher, the baker, and the rest, and took up his residence with his wife and his little children in New York. I will remark that during Harte's sojourns in Newport and Cohasset he constantly went to dinners among the fashionables where he was the only male guest whose wife had not been invited. There are some harsh terms in our language but I am not acquainted with any that is harsh enough to properly characterize a husband who will act like that.

When Harte had been living in New York two or three months he came to Hartford and stopped over night with us. He said he was without money, and without a prospect; that he owed the New York butcher and baker two hundred and fifty dollars and could get no further credit from them; also he was in debt for his rent and his landlord was threatening to turn his little family into the street. He had come to me to ask for a loan of two hundred and fifty dollars. I said that that would relieve only the butcher and baker part of the situation, with the landlord still hanging over him; he would better accept five hundred, which he did. He employed the rest of his visit in delivering himself of sparkling sarcasms about our house, our furniture, and the rest of our domestic arrangements.

Howells was saying yesterday that Harte was one of the most delightful persons he had ever met and one of the wittiest. He said that there was a charm about him that made a person forget, for the time being, his meannesses, his shabbinesses and his dishonesties, and almost forgive them. Howells is right about Harte's bright wit but he had probably never made a search into the character of it. The character of it spoiled it; it possessed no breadth and no variety; it consisted solely of sneers and sarcasms; when there was nothing to sneer at, Harte did not flash and sparkle and was not more entertaining than the rest of us.

Once he wrote a play with a perfectly delightful Chinaman in it—a play which would have succeeded if anyone else had written it; but Harte had earned the enmity of the New York dramatic critics by freely and frequently charging them with being persons who never said a favorable thing about a new play except when the favorable thing was bought and paid for beforehand. The critics were waiting for him, and when his own play was put upon the stage they attacked it with joy, they abused it and derided it remorselessly. It failed, and Harte believed that the critics were answerable for the failure. By and by he proposed that he and I should collaborate in a play in which each of us should introduce several characters and handle them. He came to Hartford and remained with us two weeks. He was a man who could never persuade himself to do a stroke of work until his credit was gone, and all his money, and the wolf was at his door; then he could sit down and work harder—until temporary relief was secured—than any man I have ever seen.

To digress for a moment. He came to us once just upon the verge of Christmas, to stay a day and finish a short story for the New York Sun called "Faithful Blossom"—if my memory serves me. He was to have a hundred and fifty dollars for the story in any case, but Mr. Dana had said he should have two hundred and fifty if he finished it in time for Christmas use. Harte had reached the middle of his story, but his time limit was now so brief that he could afford no interruptions, wherefore he had come to us to get away from the persistent visits of his creditors.

He arrived about dinner time. He said his time was so short that he must get to work straightway after dinner; then he went on chatting in serenity and comfort all through dinner, and afterward by the fire in the library until ten o'clock; then Mrs. Clemens went to bed, and my hot whisky punch was brought; also a duplicate of it for Harte. The chatting continued. I generally consume only one hot whisky, and allow myself until eleven o'clock for this function; but Harte kept on pouring and pouring, and consuming and consuming, until one o'clock; then I excused myself and said good night. He asked if he could have a bottle of whisky in his room. We rang up George and he furnished it. It seemed to me that he had already swallowed whisky enough to incapacitate him for work but it was not so; moreover, there were no signs upon him that his whisky had had a dulling effect upon his brain.

He went to his room and worked the rest of the night, with his bottle of whisky and a big wood fire for comfort. At five or six in the morning he rang for George; his bottle was empty, and he ordered another; between then and nine he drank the whole of the added quart, and then came to breakfast not drunk, not even tipsy, but quite himself and alert and animated. His story was finished; finished within the time limit, and the extra hundred dollars was secured. I wondered what a story would be like that had been completed in circumstances like these; an hour later I was to find out.

At ten o'clock the young girls' club—by name The Saturday Morning Club—arrived in our library. I was booked to talk to the lassies, but I asked Harte to take my place and read his story. He began it but it was soon plain that he was like most other people—he didn't know how to read; therefore I took it from him and read it myself. The last half of that story was written under the unpromising conditions which I have described; it is a story which I have never seen mentioned in print and I think it is quite unknown, but it is my conviction that it belongs at the very top of Harte's literature.

To go back to that other visit. The next morning after his arrival we went to the billiard room and began work upon the play. I named my characters and described them; Harte did the same by his. Then he began to sketch the scenario, act by act, and scene by scene. He worked rapidly and seemed to be troubled by no hesitations or indecisions; what he accomplished in an hour or two would have cost me several weeks of painful and difficult labor, and would have been valueless when I got through. But Harte's work was good and usable; to me it was a wonderful performance.

Then the filling in began. Harte set down the dialogue swiftly, and I had nothing to do except when one of my characters was to say something; then Harte told me the nature of the remark that was required, I furnished the language and he jotted it down. After this fashion we worked two or three or four hours every day for a couple of weeks, and produced a comedy that was good and would act. His part of it was the best part of it but that did not disturb the critics; when the piece was staged they praised my share of the work with a quite suspicious prodigality of approval, and gave Harte's share all the vitriol they had in stock. The piece perished.

All that fortnight at our house Harte made himself liberally entertaining at breakfast, at luncheon, at dinner, and in the billiard room—which was our workshop—with smart and bright sarcasms leveled at everything on the place; and for Mrs. Clemens's sake I endured it all until the last day; then, in the billiard room, he contributed the last feather; it seemed to be a slight and vague and veiled satirical remark with Mrs. Clemens for a target; he denied that she was meant, and I might have accepted the denial if I had been in a friendly mood but I was not, and was too strongly moved to give his reasonings a fair hearing. I said in substance this:

"Harte, your wife is all that is fine and lovable and lovely, and I exhaust praise when I say she is Mrs. Clemens's peer—but in all ways you are a shabby husband to her, and you often speak sarcastically, not to say sneeringly, of her, just as you are constantly doing in the case of other women; but your privilege ends there; you must spare Mrs. Clemens. It does not become you to sneer at all; you are not charged anything here for the bed you sleep in, yet you have been very smartly and wittily sarcastic about it, whereas you ought to have been more reserved in that matter, remembering that you have not owned a bed of your own for ten years; you have made sarcastic remarks about the furniture of the bedroom and about the table ware and about the servants and about the carriage and the sleigh and the coachman's livery—in fact about every detail of the house and half of its occupants; you have spoken of all these matters contemptuously, in your wholesome desire to be witty, but this does not become you; you are barred from these criticisms by your situation and circumstances;

you have a talent and a reputation which would enable you to support your family most respectably and independently if you were not a born bummer and tramp; you are a loafer and an idler, and you go clothed in rags, with not a whole shred on you except your inflamed red tie, and it isn't paid for; nine-tenths of your income is borrowed money—money which, in fact, is stolen, since you never intended to repay any of it; you sponge upon your hard-working widowed sister for bread and shelter in the mechanics' boarding-house which she keeps; latterly you have not ventured to show your face in her neighborhood because of the creditors who are on watch for you. Where have you lived? Nobody knows. Your own people do not know. But I know. You have lived in the Jersey woods and marshes, and have supported yourself as do the other tramps; you have confessed it without a blush; you sneer at everything in this house, but you ought to be more tender, remembering that everything in it was honestly come by and has been paid for."

Hart owed me fifteen hundred dollars at that time; later he owed me three thousand. He offered me his note, but I was not keeping a museum and didn't take it.

Harte's indifference concerning contracts and engagements was phenomenal. He could be blithe and gay with a broken engagement hanging over him; he could even joke about the matter; if that kind of a situation ever troubled him, the fact was not discoverable by anybody. He entered into an engagement to write the novel, *Gabriel Conroy,* for my Hartford publisher, Bliss. It was to be published by subscription. With the execution of the contract, Bliss's sorrows began. The precious time wasted along; Bliss could get plenty of promises out of Harte but no manuscript—at least no manuscript while Harte had money or could borrow it. He couldn't touch the pen until the wolf actually had him by the hind leg; then he would do two or three days' violent work and let Bliss have it for an advance of royalties.

About once a month Harte would get into desperate straits; then he would dash off enough manuscript to set him temporarily free and carry it to Bliss and get a royalty advance. These assaults upon his prospective profits were never very large, except in the eyes of Bliss; to Bliss's telescopic vision a couple of hundred dollars that weren't due, or hadn't been earned, were a prodigious matter. By and by Bliss became alarmed. In the beginning he had recognized that a contract for a full-grown novel from Bret Harte was a valuable prize, and he had been indiscreet enough to let his good fortune be trumpeted about the country. The trumpeting could have been valuable for Bliss if he had been dealing with a man addicted to keeping his engagements; but he was not dealing with that kind of a man, therefore the influence of the trumpeting had died down and vanished away long before Harte had arrived at the middle of his book; that kind of an interest once dead is dead beyond resurrection.

Finally Bliss realized that *Gabriel Conroy* was a white elephant. The book was nearing a finish, but, as a subscription book, its value had almost disappeared. He had advanced to Harte thus far—I think my figures are correct—thirty-six hundred dollars, and he knew that he should not be able to sleep much until he could find some way to make that loss good; so he sold the serial rights in *Gabriel Conroy* to one of the magazines for that trifling sum—and a good trade it was, for the serial rights were not really worth that money, and the book rights were hardly worth the duplicate of it.

I think the sense of shame was left out of Harte's

constitution. He told me once, apparently as an incident of no importance—a mere casual reminiscence—that in his early days in California when he was a blooming young chap with the world before him and bread and butter to seek, he kept a woman who was twice his age—no, the woman kept him. When he was consul in Great Britain, twenty-five or thirty years later, he was kept, at different times, by a couple of women—a connection which has gone into history, along with the names of those women. He lived in their houses, and in the house of one of them he died.

When our play was in a condition to be delivered to Parsloe, the lessee of it, I had occasion to go to New York, and I stopped at the St. James Hotel, as usual. Harte had been procrastinating; the play should have been in Parsloe's hands a day or two earlier than this, but Harte had not attended to it. About seven in the evening he came into the lobby of the hotel, dressed in an ancient gray suit so out of repair that the bottoms of his trousers were frazzled to a fringe; his shoes were similarly out of repair and were sodden with snow-slush and mud, and on his head and slightly tipped to starboard rested a crumpled little soft hat which was a size or two too small for him; his bright little red necktie was present, and rather more than usually cheery and contented and conspicuous. He had the play in his hand. Parsloe's theatre was not three minutes' walk distant; I supposed he would say, "Come along—let's take the play to Parsloe."

But he didn't; he stepped up to the counter, offered his parcel to the clerk, and said with the manner of an earl, "It is for Mr. Parsloe—send it to the theater."

The clerk looked him over austerely and said, with the air of a person who is presenting a checkmating difficulty,

"The messenger's fee will be ten cents."

Harte said, "Call him."

Which the clerk did. The boy answered the call, took the parcel and stood waiting for orders. There was a certain malicious curiosity visible in the clerk's face. Harte turned toward me, and said, "Let me have a dollar."

I handed it to him. He handed it to the boy and said, "Run along."

The clerk said, "Wait, I'll give you the change."

Harte gave his hand a ducal wave and said, "Never mind it. Let the boy keep it."

Harte had no feeling, for the reason that he had no machinery to feel with. John McCullough, the tragedian, was a man of high character; a generous man, a lovable man, and a man whose truthfulness could not be challenged. He was a great admirer of Harte's literature, and in the early days in San Francisco he had had a warm fondness for Harte himself; as the years went by this fondness cooled to some extent, a circumstance for which Hart was responsible. However, in the days of Harte's consulship McCullough's affection for him had merely undergone a diminution; it had by no means disappeared; but by and by something happened which abolished what was left of it. John McCullough told me all about it.

One day a young man appeared in his quarters in New York, and said he was Bret Harte's son, and had just arrived from England with a letter of introduction and recommendation from his father—and he handed the letter to McCullough. McCullough greeted him cordially, and said, "I was expecting you, my boy. I know your errand, through a letter which I have already received from your father; and by good lick I am in a position to satisfy your desire. I have just the place for you, and you can consider yourself on salary from today, and now."

Young Harte was eloquently grateful, and said, "I knew you would be expecting me, for my father promised me that he would write you in advance."

McCullough had Harte's letter in his pocket but he did not read it to the lad. In substance it was this:

"My boy is stage-struck and wants to go to you for help, for he knows that you and I are old friends. To get rid of his importunities, I have been obliged to start him across the water equipped with a letter strongly recommending him to your kindness and protection, and begging you to do the best you can to forward his ambition, for my sake. I was obliged to write the letter, I couldn't get out of it, but the present letter is to warn you beforehand to pay no attention to the other one. My son is stage-struck, but he isn't of any account, and will never amount to anything; therefore don't bother yourself with him; it wouldn't pay you for your lost time and sympathy."

John McCullough stood by the boy and pushed his fortunes on the stage and was the best father the lad ever had.

I have said more than once in these pages that Harte had no heart and no conscience, and I have also said that he was mean and base. I have not said, perhaps, that he was treacherous, but if I have omitted that remark I wish to add it now.

All of us at one time or another blunder stupidly into indiscreet acts and speeches; I am not an exception; I have done it myself. About a dozen years ago, I drifted into the Players Club one night and found half a dozen of the boys grouped cozily in a private corner sipping punches and talking. I joined them and assisted. Presently Bret Harte's name was mentioned and straightway that mention fired a young fellow who sat at my elbow, and for the next ten minutes he talked as only a person can talk whose subject lies near his heart. Nobody interrupted; everybody was interested. The young fellow's talk was made up of strong and genuine enthusiasms; its subject was praise—praise of Mrs. Harte and her daughters. He told how they were living in a little town in New Jersey, and how hard they worked, and how faithfully, and how cheerfully, and how contentedly, to earn their living—Mrs. Harte by teaching music, the daughters by exercising the arts of drawing, embroidery, and such things—I meantime listening as eagerly as the rest, for I was aware that he was speaking the truth and not overstating it.

But presently he diverged into eulogies of the ostensible head of that deserted family, Bret Harte. He said that the family's happiness had one defect in it; the absence of Harte. He said that their love and their reverence for him was a beautiful thing to see and hear; also their pity of him on account of his enforced exile from home. He also said that Harte's own grief, because of this bitter exile, was beautiful to contemplate; that Harte's faithfulness in writing by every steamer was beautiful, too; that he was always longing to come home in his vacations but his salary was so small that he could not afford it; nevertheless, in his letters he was always promising himself this happiness in the next steamer or the next one after that one; and that it was pitiful to see the family's disappointment when the named steamer kept on arriving without him; that his self-sacrifice was an ennobling spectacle; that he was man enough and fine enough to deny himself in order that he might send to the family every month, for their support, that portion of his salary which a more selfish person would devote to the Atlantic voyage.

Up to this time I had "stood the raise," as the poker players say, but now I broke out and called the young fellow's hand—as the poker players also say. I couldn't help it, I saw that he had been misinformed. It seemed to be my duty to set him right.

I said, "Oh, that be hanged! There's nothing in it. Bret Harte has deserted his family, and that is the plain English of it. Possibly he writes to them, but I am not weak enough to believe it until I see the letters; possibly he is pining to come home to his deserted family, but no one that knows him will believe that. But there is one thing about which I think there can be no possibility of doubt—and that is, that he has never sent them a dollar, and has never intended to send them a dollar. Bret Harte is the most contemptible, poor little soulless blatherskite that exists on the planet today—"

I had been dimly aware, very vaguely aware, by fitful glimpses of the countenances around me, that something was happening. It was I that was happening, but I didn't know it.

But when I had reached the middle of that last sentence somebody seized me and whispered into my ear, with energy, "For goodness sake shut up! This young fellow is Steele. He's engaged to one of the daughters."

—1907

On Publishing

The Jumping Frog

My experiences as an author began early in 1867. I came to New York from San Francisco in the first month of that year and presently Charles H. Webb, whom I had known in San Francisco as a reporter on *The Bulletin* and afterward editor of *The Californian*, suggested that I publish a volume of sketches. I had but a slender reputation to publish it on, but I was charmed and excited by the suggestion and quite willing to venture it if some industrious person would save me the trouble of gathering the sketches together. I was loath to do it myself, for from the beginning of my sojourn in this world there was a persistent vacancy in me where the industry ought to be.

Webb said I had some reputation in the Atlantic states but I knew quite well that it must be of a very attenuated sort. What there was of it rested upon the story of "The Jumping Frog." When Artemus Ward passed through California on a lecturing tour in 1865 or '66, I told him the "Jumping Frog" story in San Francisco and he asked me to write it out and send it to his publisher, Carleton, in New York, to be used in padding out a small book which Artemus had prepared for the press and which needed some more stuffing to make it big enough for the price which was to be charged for it.

It reached Carleton in time, but he didn't think much of it and was not willing to go to the typesetting expense of adding it to the book. He did not put it in the wastebasket, but made Henry Clapp a present of it, and Clapp used it to help out the funeral of his dying literary journal, *The Saturday Press.* "The Jumping Frog" appeared in the last number of that paper, and was at once copied in the newspapers of America and England. It certainly had a wide celebrity and it still had it at the time that I am speaking of—but I was aware that it was only the frog that was celebrated. It wasn't I. I was still an obscurity.

Webb undertook to collate the sketches. He performed this office, then handed the result to me, and I went to Carleton's establishment with it. I approached a clerk and he bent eagerly over the counter to inquire into my needs; but when he found that I had come to sell a book and not to buy one, his temperature fell sixty degrees and I came near to freezing where I stood. I meekly asked the privilege of a word with Mr. Carleton, and was coldly informed that he was in his private office. Discouragements and difficulties followed, but after a while I got by the frontier and entered the Holy of Holies. Ah, now I remember how I managed it! Webb had made an appointment for me with Carleton; otherwise I never should have gotten over that frontier. Carleton rose and said brusquely and aggressively, "Well, what can I do for you?"

I reminded him that I was there by appointment to offer him my book for publication. He began to swell, and went on swelling and swelling and swelling until he had reached the dimensions of a god of about the second or third degree. Then the fountains of his great deep were broken up, and for two or three minutes I couldn't see him for the rain. It was words, only words, but they fell so densely that they darkened the atmosphere. Finally he made an imposing sweep with his right hand which comprehended the whole room and said, "Books—look at those shelves. Every one of them is loaded with books that are waiting for publication. Do I want any more? Excuse me, I don't. Good morning."

Twenty-one years elapsed before I saw Carleton again. I was then sojourning with my family at the Schweizerhof, in Lucerne. He called on me, shook hands cordially, and said at once without any preliminaries, "I am substantially an obscure person, but I have a couple of such colossal distinctions to my credit that I am entitled to immortality—to wit: I refused a book of yours and for this I stand without competitor as the prize ass of the nineteenth century."

It was a most handsome apology, and I told him so and said it was a long delayed revenge but was sweeter to me than any other that could be devised, that during the lapsed twenty-one years I had in fancy taken his life several times every year and always in new and increasingly malignant ways, but that now I was pacified, appeased, happy, even jubilant, and that thenceforth I should hold him my true and valued friend and never kill him again.

I reported my adventure to Webb and he bravely said that not all the Carletons in the universe should defeat that book, he would publish it himself on a ten per cent royalty. And so he did. He brought it out in blue and gold, and made a very pretty little book of it. I think he named it *The Celebrated Jumping Frog of Calaveras County, and Other Sketches*, price $1.25. He made the plates and printed and bound the book through a job printing house and published it through the American News Company.

In June I sailed in the *Quaker City* Excursion. I returned in November, and in Washington found a letter from Elisha Bliss of the American Publishing Company of Hartford, offering me five per cent royalty on a book which should recount the adventures of the Excursion. In lieu of the royalty I was offered the alternative of ten thousand dollars cash upon delivery of the manuscript. I consulted A. D. Richardson and he said "Take the royalty." I followed his advice and closed with Bliss. By my contract I was to deliver the manuscript in July of 1868. I wrote the book in San Francisco and delivered the manuscript within contract time. Bliss provided a multitude of illustrations for the book and then stopped. The contract date for the issue of the book went by and there was no explanation of this. Time drifted along and still there was no explanation. I was lecturing all over the country; and about thirty times a day, on an average, I was trying to answer this question: "When is your book coming out?" I got tired of inventing new answers to that question, and by and by I got horribly tired of the question itself. Whoever asked it became my enemy at once and I was usually almost eager to make that appear.

As soon as I was free of the lecture field I hastened to Hartford to make inquiries. Bliss said that the fault was not his. He wanted to publish the book but the directors of his company were staid old fogies and they were afraid of it. They had examined the book and the majority of them were of the opinion that there were places in it of a humorous character. Bliss said the house had never published a book that had a suspicion like that attaching to it, and that the directors were afraid that a departure of this kind could seriously injure the house's reputation, that he was tied hand and foot and was not permitted to carry out his contract.

One of the directors, a Mr. Drake—at least he was the remains of what had once been a Mr. Drake—invited me to take a ride with him in his buggy and I went along. He was a pathetic old relic and his ways and his talk were also pathetic. He had a delicate purpose in view and it took him some time to hearten himself sufficiently to carry it out, but at last he accomplished it. He explained the house's difficulty and distress, as Bliss had already explained it.

Then he frankly threw himself and the house upon my mercy and begged me to take away *The Innocents Abroad* and release the concern from the contract. I said I wouldn't—and so ended the interview and the buggy excursion.

Then I warned Bliss that he must get to work or I should make trouble. He acted upon the warning and set up the book and I read the proofs. Then there was another long wait and no explanation. At last toward the end of July (1869, I think) I lost patience and telegraphed Bliss that if the book was not on sale in twenty-four hours I should bring suit for damages. That ended the trouble. Half a dozen copies were bound and placed on sale within the required time. Then the canvassing began, and went briskly forward. In nine months the book took the publishing house out of debt, advanced its stock from twenty-five to two hundred, and left seventy thousand dollars profit to the good. It was Bliss that told me this—but if it was true it was the first time that Bliss had told the truth in sixty-five years. He was born in 1804.

—1906

The American Publishing Company

But I must go back to [Charles H.] Webb. When I got back from the *Quaker City* Excursion, in November, 1867, Webb told me that *The Jumping Frog* book had been favorably received by the press and that he believed it had sold fairly well, but that he had found it impossible to get a statement of account from the American News Company. He said the book had been something of a disaster to him, since he had manufactured it with his own private funds and was now not able to get any of the money back because of the dishonest and dodging ways of the News Company.

I was very sincerely sorry for Webb, sorry that he had lost money by befriending me, also in some degree sorry that he was not able to pay me my royalties.

I made my contract for *The Innocents Abroad* with the American Publishing Company. Then after two or three months had gone by it occurred to me that perhaps I was violating that contract, there being a clause in it forbidding me to publish books with any other firm during a term of a year or so. Of course that clause could not cover a book which had been published before the contract was made; anybody else would have known that. But I didn't know it, for I was not in the habit of knowing anything that was valuable and I was also not in the habit of asking other people for information.

It was my ignorant opinion that I was violating the Bliss contract and that I was in honor bound to suppress

The Jumping Frog book and take it permanently out of print. So I went to Webb with the matter. He was willing to accommodate me upon these terms: that I should surrender to him such royalties as might be due me; that I should also surrender to him, free of royalty, all bound and unbound copies which might be in the News Company's hands; also that I should hand him eight hundred dollars cash; also that he should superintend the breaking up of the plates of the book, and for that service should receive such bounty as the type founders should pay for the broken plates as old type metal. Type metal was worth nine cents a pound and the weight of the plates was about forty pounds. One may perceive by these details that Webb had some talent as a trader.

After this Webb passed out of the field of my vision for a long time. But meantime chance threw me in the way of the manager of the American News Company, and I asked him about Webb's difficulties with the concern and how they had come about. He said he didn't know of any difficulties. I then explained to him that Webb had never been able to collect anything from the company. In turn, he explained to me that my explanation was not sound. He said the company had always furnished statements to Webb at the usual intervals, and had accompanied them with the company's check to date. By his invitation I went with him to his office, and by his books and accounts he proved to me that what he had said was true. Webb had collected his dues and mine regularly from the beginning and had pocketed the money. At the time that Webb and I had settled, he was owing me six hundred dollars on royalties. The bound and unbound *Jumping Frogs* which he had inherited from me at that time had since been sold, and the result had gone into his pocket—part of it being six hundred more that should have come to me on royalties.

To sum up, I was now an author, I was an author with some little trifle of reputation, I was an author who had published a book, I was an author who had not become rich through that publication, I was an author whose first book had cost him twelve hundred dollars in unreceived royalties, eight hundred dollars in blood money, and three dollars and sixty cents smouched from old type metal. I was resolved from that moment that I would not publish with Webb any more—unless I could borrow money enough to support the luxury.

By and by when I became notorious through the publication of *The Innocents Abroad*, Webb was able to satisfy the public, first that he had discovered me, later that he had created me. It was quite generally conceded that I was a valuable asset to the American nation and to the great ranks of literature, also that for the acquisition of this asset a deep debt of gratitude was due from the nation and the ranks—to Webb.

By and by Webb and his high service were forgotten. Then Bliss and the American Publishing Company came forward and established the fact that they had discovered me, later that they had created me, therefore that some more gratitude was due. In the course of time there were still other claimants for these great services. They sprang up in California, Nevada, and around generally, and I came at last to believe that I had been more multitudinously discovered and created than any other animal that had ever issued from the Deity's hands.

Webb believed that he was a literary person. He might have gotten this superstition accepted by the world if he had not extinguished it by publishing his things. They gave him away. His prose was enchantingly puerile, his poetry was not any better, yet he kept on grinding out his commonplaces at intervals until he died, two years ago, of over-cerebration. He was a poor sort of a creature and by nature and training a fraud. As a liar he was well enough and had some success but no distinction, because he was a contemporary of Elisha Bliss and when it came to lying Bliss could overshadow and blot out a whole continent of Webbs like a total eclipse.

About 1872 I wrote another book, *Roughing It.* I had published *The Innocents* on a five per cent royalty, which would amount to about twenty-two cents per volume. Proposals were coming in now from several other good houses. One offered fifteen per cent royalty; another offered to give me *all* of the profits and be content with the advertisement which the book would furnish the house. I sent for Bliss and he came to Elmira. If I had known as much about book publishing then as I know now, I would have required of Bliss seventy-five or eighty per cent of the profits above cost of manufacture, and this would have been fair and just. But I knew nothing about the business and had been too indolent to try to learn anything about it. I told Bliss I did not wish to leave his corporation, and that I did not want extravagant terms. I said I thought I ought to have half the profit above cost of manufacture and he said with enthusiasm that that was exactly right, exactly right.

He went to his hotel and drew the contract and brought it to the house in the afternoon. I found a difficulty in it. It did not name "half profits," but named a seven and a half per cent royalty instead. I asked him to explain that. I said that was not the understanding. He said "No, it wasn't," but that he had put in a royalty to simplify the matter—that seven and a half per cent royalty represented fully half the profit and a little more, up to a sale of a hundred thousand copies, that after that the publishing company's half would be a shade superior to mine.

I was a little doubtful, a little suspicious, and asked him if he could swear to that. He promptly put up his hand and made oath to it, exactly repeating the words which he had just used.

It took me nine or ten years to find out that that was a false oath, and that seven and a half per cent did not represent one-fourth of the profits. But in the meantime I had published several books with Bliss on seven and a half and ten per cent royalties, and of course had been handsomely swindled on all of them.

In 1879 I came home from Europe with a book ready for the press, *A Tramp Abroad*. I sent for Bliss and he came out to the house to discuss the book. I said that I was not satisfied about those royalties and that I did not believe in their "half-profit" pretenses, that this time he must put the "half profit" in the contract and make no mention of royalties—otherwise I would take the book elsewhere. He said he was perfectly willing to put it in, for it was right and just, and that if his directors opposed it and found fault with it he would withdraw from the concern and publish the book himself—fine talk, but I knew that he was master in that concern and that it would have to accept any contract that had been signed by him. This contract lay there on the billiard table with his signature attached to it. He had ridden his directors roughshod ever since the days of *The Innocents Abroad* and more than once he had told me that he had made his directors do things which they hadn't wanted to do, with the threat that if they did not comply he would leave the company's service and take me along with him.

I don't know how a grown person could ever be so simple and innocent as I was in those days. It ought to have occurred to me that a man who could talk like that must either be a fool or convinced that I was one.

However, I was the one. And so even very simple and rudimentary wisdoms were not likely to find their way into my head.

I reminded him that his company would not be likely to make any trouble about a contract which had been signed by him. Then, with one of his toothless smiles, he pointed out a detail which I had overlooked, to wit: the contract was with Elisha Bliss, a private individual, and the American Publishing Company was not mentioned in it.

He told me afterward that he took the contract to the directors and said that he would turn it over to the company for one-fourth of the profits of the book together with an increase of salary for himself and for Frank, his son, and that if these terms were not satisfactory he would leave the company and publish the book himself, whereupon the directors granted his demands and took the contract. The fact that Bliss told me these things with his own mouth is unassailable evidence that they were not true. Six weeks before the book issued from the press Bliss told the truth once, to see how it would taste, but it overstrained him and he died.

When the book had been out three months there was an annual meeting of the stockholders of the company and I was present, as a half-partner in the book. The meeting was held in the house of a neighbor of mine, Newton Case, a director in the company from the beginning. A statement of the company's business was read, and to me it was a revelation. Sixty-four thousand copies of the book had been sold, and my half of the profit was thirty-two thousand dollars. In 1872 Bliss had made out to me that seven and a half per cent royalty, some trifle over twenty cents a copy, represented one-half of the profits, whereas at that earlier day it hardly represented a sixth of the profits. Times were not so good now, yet it took all of fifty cents a copy to represent half.

Well, Bliss was dead and I couldn't settle with him for his ten years of swindlings. He has been dead a quarter of a century now. My bitterness against him has faded away and disappeared. I feel only compassion for him and if I could send him a fan I would.

When the balance sheets exposed to me the rascalities which I had been suffering at the hands of the American Publishing Company I stood up and delivered a lecture to Newton Case and the rest of the conspirators—meaning the rest of the directors.

—1906

Setting Up as a Publisher

As I have already remarked [in other writings], I had imported my nephew-in-law, [Charles] Webster, from the village of Dunkirk, New York, to conduct that original first patent-right business for me, at a salary of fifteen hundred dollars. That enterprise had lost forty-two thousand dollars for me, so I thought this a favorable time to close it up. I proposed to be my own publisher now and let young Webster do the work. He thought he ought to have twenty-five hundred dollars a year while he was learning the trade. I took a day or two to consider the matter and study it out searchingly. So far as I could see, this was a new idea. I remembered that printers' apprentices got *no* salary. Upon inquiry I found that this was the case with stone masons, brick masons, tinners, and the rest. I found that not even lawyers or apprenticed doctors got any salary for learning the trade. I remembered that on the river an apprentice pilot not only got nothing in the way of salary but he also had to pay some pilot a sum in cash which he didn't have—a large sum. It was what I had done myself. I had paid Bixby a hundred dollars and it was borrowed money. I was told by a person who said he was studying for the ministry that even Noah got no salary for the first six months—partly on account of the weather and partly because he was learning navigation.

The upshot of these thinkings and searchings of mine was that I believed I had secured something entirely new to history in Webster. And also I believed that a young backwoodsman who was starting life in New York without equipment of any kind, without proved value of any kind, without prospective value of any kind, yet able without blinking an eye to propose to learn a trade at another man's expense and charge for this benefaction an annual sum greater than any president of the United States had ever been able to save out of his pay for running the most difficult country on the planet, after Ireland, must surely be worth securing—and instantly—lest he get away. I believed that if some of his gigantic interest in No. 1 could be diverted to the protection of No. 2, the result would be fortune enough for me.

I erected Webster into a firm—a firm entitled Webster and Company, Publishers—and installed him in a couple of offices at a modest rental on the second floor of a building somewhere below Union Square, I don't remember where. For assistants he had a girl and perhaps a masculine clerk of about eight-hundred-dollar size. For a while Webster had another helper. This was a man who had long been in the subscription-book business, knew all about it, and was able to teach it to Webster—which he did—I paying the cost of tuition. I am talking about the early part of 1884 now. I handed Webster a competent capital and along with it I handed him the manuscript of *Huckleberry Finn*. Webster's function was general agent. It was his business to appoint sub-agents throughout the country. At that time there were sixteen of these sub-agencies. They had canvassers under them who did the canvassing. In New York City Webster was his own sub-agent.

Before ever any of these minor details that I am talking about had entered into being, the careful Webster had suggested that a contract be drawn and signed and sealed before we made any real move. That seemed sane, though I should not have thought of it myself—I mean it *was* sane *because* I had not thought of it myself. So Webster got his own lawyer to draw the contract. I was coming to admire Webster very much, and at this point in the proceedings I had one of those gushing generosities surge up in my system, and before I had thought, I had tried to confer upon Webster a tenth interest in the business in addition to his salary, free of charge. Webster declined promptly—with thanks, of course, the usual kind. That raised him another step in my admiration. I knew perfectly well that I was offering him a partnership interest which would pay him two or three times his salary within the next nine months, but he didn't know that. He was coldly and wisely discounting all my prophecies about *Huckleberry Finn's* high commercial value. And here was this new evidence that in Webster I had found a jewel, a man who would not get excited; a man who would not lose his head; a cautious man; a man who would not take a risk of any kind in fields unknown to him. Except at somebody else's expense, I mean.

The contract was drawn, as I say, by a young lawyer from Dunkirk, New York, which produced him as well as Webster, and has not yet gotten over the strain. Whitford was privileged to sign himself "of the firm of Alexander and Green." Alexander and Green had a great and lucrative business and not enough conscience to damage it—a fact which came out rather prominently last year when the earthquake came which shook the entrails out of the three great life insurance companies. Alexander and Green had their offices in the Mutual Building. They kept a job lot of twenty-five lawyers on salary, and he was one of these. He was good-natured, obliging, and immensely ignorant, and was endowed with a stupidity which by the least little stretch would go around the globe four times and tie.

That first contract was all right. There was nothing the matter with it. It placed all obligations, all expenses, all liability, all responsibilities upon *me*, where they belonged.

It was a happy combination, Webster and his lawyer. The amount that the two together didn't know about anything was to me a much more awful and paralyzing spectacle than it would be to see the Milky Way get wrecked and drift off in rags and patches through the sky. When it came to courage, moral or physical, they hadn't any. Webster was afraid to venture anything in the way of business without first getting a lawyer's assurance that there was nothing jailable about it. Lawyer was consulted so nearly constantly that he was about as much a member of the staff as was the girl and the subscription expert. But as neither Webster nor he had had any personal experience of money, his lawyer was not an expensive incumbent, though he probably thought he was.

At the break of the autumn I went off with George W. Cable on a four months' reading campaign in the East and West—the last platform work which I was ever to do in this life in my own country. I resolved at the time that I would never rob the public from the platform again unless driven to it by pecuniary compulsions. After eleven years the pecuniary compulsions came and I lectured all around the globe.

Ten years have since elapsed, during which time I have only lectured for public charities and without pay. On the 19th of last month I took a public and formal leave of the platform—a thing which I had not done before—in a lecture on Robert Fulton for the benefit of the Robert Fulton Monument Fund.

I seem to be getting pretty far away from Webster and Whitford, but it's no matter. It is one of those cases where distance lends enchantment to the view. Webster was successful with *Huckleberry Finn*, and a year later handed me the firm's check for fifty-four thousand five hundred dollars, which included the fifteen thousand dollars capital which I had originally handed to him.

Once more I experienced a new birth. I have been born more times than anybody except Krishna, I suppose.

—1906

General Grant's Publisher

Webster [Clemens's nephew-in-law] conceived the idea that he had discovered me to the world but he was reasonably modest about it. He did much less cackling over his egg than Webb and Bliss had done.

It had never been my intention to publish anybody's books but my own. An accident diverted me from this wise purpose. That was General Grant's memorable book. One night in the first week of November, 1884, I had been lecturing in Chickering Hall and was walking homeward. It was a rainy night and but few people were about. In the midst of a black gulf between lamps, two dim figures stepped out of a doorway and moved along in front of me. I heard one of them say, "Do you know General Grant has actually determined to write his memoirs and publish them? He has said so today, in so many words."

That was all I heard—just those words—and I thought it great good luck that I was permitted to overhear them.

In the morning I went out and called on General Grant. I found him in his library with Col. Fred Grant, his son. The General said in substance this: "Sit down and keep quiet until I sign a contract"—and added that it was for a book which he was going to write.

Fred Grant was apparently conducting a final reading and examination of the contract himself. He found it satisfactory and said so, and his father stepped to the table and took up the pen. It might have been better for me, possibly, if I had let him alone but I didn't. I said, "Don't sign it. Let Col. Fred read it to me first."

Col. Fred read it, and I said I was glad I had come in time to interfere. The Century Company was the party of the second part. It proposed to pay the General ten per cent royalty. Of course this was nonsense—but the proposal had its source in ignorance, not dishonesty. The great Century Company knew all about magazine publishing. No one could teach them anything about that industry. But at that time they had had no experience of subscription publishing, and they probably had nothing in their minds except trade publishing. They could not even have had any valuable experience in trade publishing, or they would not have asked General Grant to furnish a book on the royalty commonly granted to authors of no name or repute.

I explained that these terms would never do; that they were all wrong, unfair, unjust. I said, "Strike out the ten per cent and put twenty per cent in its place. Better still, put seventy-five per cent of the net returns in its place."

The General demurred, and quite decidedly. He said they would never pay those terms.

I said that that was a matter of no consequence, since there was not a reputable publisher in America who would not be very glad to pay them.

The General still shook his head. He was still desirous of signing the contract as it stood.

I pointed out that the contract as it stood had an offensive detail in it which I had never heard of in the ten per cent contract of even the most obscure author—that this contract not only proposed a ten per cent royalty for such a colossus as General Grant, but it also had in it a requirement that out of that ten per cent must come some trivial tax for the book's share of clerk hire, house rent, sweeping out the offices, or some such nonsense as that. I said he ought to have three-fourths of the profits and let the publisher pay running expenses out of his remaining fourth.

The idea distressed General Grant. He thought it placed him in the attitude of a robber—robber of a publisher. I said that if he regarded that as a crime it was because his education was limited. I said it was not a crime and was always rewarded in heaven with two halos. Would be, if it ever happened.

The General was immovable and challenged me to name the publisher that would be willing to have this noble deed perpetrated upon him. I named the American Publishing Company of Hartford. He asked if I could prove my position. I said I could furnish the proof by telegraph in six hours—three hours for my despatch to go to Hartford, three hours for Bliss's jubilant acceptance to return by the same electric gravel train—that if he needed this answer quicker I would walk up to Hartford and fetch it.

The General still stood out. But Fred Grant was beginning to be persuaded. He proposed that the Century contract be laid on the table for twenty-four hours and that meantime the situation be examined and discussed. He said that this thing was not a matter of sentiment; it was a matter of pure business and should be examined from that point of view alone. His remark about sentiment had a bearing. The reason was this. The broking firm of Grant and Ward—consisting of General Grant, Mr. Ward (called for a time the "Little Napoleon of Finance") and Ward's confederate, Fish—had swindled General Grant out of every penny he had in the world. And at a time when he did not know where to turn for bread, Roswell Smith, head of the Century Company, offered him five hundred dollars per article for four magazine articles about certain great battles of the Civil War. The offer came to the despairing old hero like the fabled straw to the drowning man. He accepted it with gratitude and wrote the articles and delivered them. They were easily worth ten thousand dollars apiece but he didn't know it. Five hundred dollars apiece seemed to him fabulous pay for a trifle of pleasant and unlaborious scribbling.

He was now most loath to desert these benefactors of his. To his military mind and training it seemed disloyalty. If I remember rightly his first article lifted the Century's subscription list from a hundred thousand copies to two hundred and twenty thousand. This made the Century's advertisement pages, for that month, worth more than double the money they had ever commanded in any previous month. As a guess, I should say that this increase of patronage was worth, that month, eight thousand dollars. This is a safe estimate, a conservative estimate.

The doubled subscription list established in that month was destined to continue for years. It was destined to increase the magazine's advertisement income about eight or ten thousand dollars a month during six years. I have said that each of General Grant's articles was worth ten thousand dollars instead of five hundred. I could say that each of the four articles was worth twenty-five thousand dollars and still be within bounds.

I began to tout for the American Publishing Company. I argued that the company had been first in the field as applicants for a volume of Grant memoirs and that perhaps they ought to have a chance at a bid before the Century Company. This seemed to be news to General Grant. But I reminded him that once during the apparently wonderfully prosperous days of the firm of Grant and Ward I called upon him in his private office one day, helped him to consume his luncheon, and begged him to write his memoirs and give them to the American Publishing

Company. He had declined at the time, and most decidedly, saying he was not in need of money and that he was not a literary person and could not write the memoirs.

I think we left the contract matter to stew for that time, and took it up again the next morning. I knew quite well that the American Publishing Company would be glad to get General Grant's memoirs on a basis of three-quarters profit for him, to one-quarter for themselves. Indeed I knew quite well that there was not a publisher in the country—I mean a publisher experienced in the subscription publishing business—who would not be glad to get the book on those terms. I was fully expecting to presently hand that book to Frank Bliss and the American Publishing Company and enrich that den of reptiles—but the sober second thought came then. I reflected that the company had been robbing me for years and building theological factories out of the proceeds, and that now was my chance to feed fat the ancient grudge I bore them.

At the second conference with the General and Fred, the General exhibited some of the modesty which was so large a feature of his nature. General Sherman had published his *Memoirs* in two large volumes with Scribner's, and that publication had been a notable event. General Grant said:

"Sherman told me that his profits on that book were twenty-five thousand dollars. Do you believe I could get as much out of my book?"

I said I not only believed but I *knew* that he would achieve a vastly greater profit than that—that Sherman's book was published in the trade; that it was a suitable book for subscription distribution and ought to have been published in that way; that not many books were suitable to that method of publishing, but that the memoirs of such illustrious persons as Sherman and Grant were peculiarly adapted to that method; that a book which contained the right material for that method would harvest from eight to ten times as much profit by subscription as it could be made to produce by trade sale.

The General had his doubts that he could gather twenty-five thousand dollars profit for his memoirs. I inquired why. He said he had already applied the test and had secured the evidence and the verdict. I wondered where he could have gotten such evidence and such a verdict, and he explained. He said he had offered to sell his memoirs out and out to Roswell Smith for twenty-five thousand dollars, and that the proposition had so frightened Smith that he hardly had breath enough left in his clothes to decline with.

Then I had an idea. It suddenly occurred to me that I was a publisher myself. I had not thought of it before. I said, "Sell *me* the memoirs, General. I am a publisher. I will pay double price. I have a checkbook in my pocket; take my check for fifty thousand dollars now, and let's draw the contract."

General Grant was as prompt in declining this as Roswell Smith had been in declining the other offer. He said he wouldn't hear of such a thing. He said we were friends, and if I should fail to get the money back out of his book— He stopped there and said there was no occasion to go into particulars, he simply would not consent to help a friend run any such risk.

Then I said, "Give me the book on the terms which I have already suggested that you make with the Century people—twenty per cent royalty or in lieu of that seventy-five per cent of the profits on the publication to go to you, I to pay all running expenses such as salaries, etc., out of my fourth."

He laughed at that and asked me what my profit out of

that remnant would be. I said, a hundred thousand dollars in six months.

He was dealing with a literary person. He was aware, by authority of all the traditions, that literary persons are flighty, romantic, unpractical, and in business matters do not know enough to come in when it rains or at any other time. He did not say that he attached no value to these flights of my imagination, for he was too kindly to say hurtful things, but he might better have said it because he looked it with tenfold emphasis and the look covered the whole ground. To make conversation, I suppose, he asked me what I based this dream upon—if it had a basis.

I said, "I base it upon the difference between your literary commercial value and mine. My first two books sold a hundred and fifty thousand copies each—three dollars and a half per volume in cloth, costlier volumes at a higher price according to binding—average price of the hundred and fifty thousand, four dollars apiece. I know that your commercial value is easily four times as great as mine; therefore I know it to be a perfectly safe guess that your book will sell six hundred thousand single volumes, and that the clear profit to you will be half a million dollars and the clear profit to me a hundred thousand.

We had a long discussion over the matter. Finally General Grant telegraphed for his particular friend, George W. Childs of the Philadelphia *Ledger,* to come up to New York and furnish an opinion. Childs came. I convinced him that Webster's publishing machinery was ample and in good order. Then Childs delivered the verdict, "Give the book to Clemens." Col. Fred Grant endorsed and repeated the verdict, "Give the book to Clemens." So the contract was drawn and signed, and Webster took hold of his new job at once.

By my existing contract with Webster he merely had a

salary of twenty-five hundred dollars a year. He had declined to accept, gratis, an interest in the business, for he was a cautious person and averse from running risks. I now offered him, gratis, a tenth share in the business—the contract as to other details to remain as before. Then, as a counter proposition, he modestly offered this: that his salary be increased to thirty-five hundred dollars a year; that he have ten per cent of the profits accruing from the Grant book, and that I furnish all the capital required at seven per cent.

I said I should be satisfied with this arrangement.

Then he called in his pal, Whitford, who drew the contract. I couldn't understand the contract—I never could understand any contract—and I asked my brother-in-law, General Langdon, a trained business man, to understand it for me. He read it and said it was all right. So we signed it and sealed it. I was to find out later that the contract gave Webster ten per cent of the profits on the Grant book *and* ten per cent interest in the profits of the whole business—but not any interest in such losses as might occur.

The news went forth that General Grant was going to write his memoirs and that the firm of Charles L. Webster & Co. would publish them. The announcement produced a vast sensation throughout the country. The nation was glad and this feeling poured itself heartily out in all the newspapers. On the one day, young Webster was as unknown as the unborn babe. The next day he was a notoriety. His name was in every paper in the United States. He was young, he was human, he naturally mistook this transient notoriety for fame, and by consequence he had to get his hat enlarged. His juvenile joy in his new grandeur was a pretty and pleasant spectacle to see. The first thing he did was to move out of his modest quarters and secure quarters better suited to his new importance as the most distinguished publisher in the country.

His new quarters were on the second or third floor of a tall building which fronted on Union Square, a commercially aristocratic locality. His previous quarters had consisted of two good-sized rooms. His new ones occupied the whole floor. What Webster really needed was a cubbyhole up a back street somewhere, with room to swing a cat in—a long cat; this cubbyhole for office work. He needed no storage rooms, no cellars. The printers and binders of the great memoir took care of the sheets and the bound volumes for us and charged storage and insurance. Conspicuous quarters were not needed for that mighty book. You couldn't have hidden General Grant's publisher where the agent and the canvasser could not find him. The cubbyhole would have been sufficient for all our needs. Almost all the business would be transacted by correspondence. That correspondence would be with the sixteen general agents, none of it with their ten thousand canvassers.

However, it was a very nice spread that we made, as far as spaciousness and perspective went. These were impressive—that is, as impressive as nakedness long drawn out and plenty of it could be. It seemed to me that the look of the place was going to deceive country people and drive them away, and I suggested that we put up a protecting sign just inside the door: "Come in. It is not a rope walk."

It was a mistake to deal in sarcasms with Webster. They cut deep into his vanity. He hadn't a single intellectual weapon in his armory and could not fight back. It was unchivalrous of me to attack with mental weapons this mentally weaponless man, and I tried to refrain from it but couldn't. I ought to have been large enough to endure his vanities but I wasn't. I am not always large enough to endure my own. He had one defect which particularly exasperated me, because I didn't have it myself. When a matter was mentioned of which he was ignorant, he not only would not protect himself by remarking that he was not acquainted with the matter, but he had not even discretion enough to keep his tongue still. He would say something intended to deceive the hearers into the notion that he knew something about that subject himself—a most unlikely condition, since his ignorance covered the whole earth like a blanket and there was hardly a hole in it anywhere. Once in a drawing-room company some talk sprang up about George Eliot and her literature. I saw Webster getting ready to contribute. There was no way to hit him with a brick or a Bible or something and reduce him to unconsciousness and save him, because it would have attracted attention—therefore I waited for his mountain to bring forth its mouse, which it did as soon as there was a vacancy between speeches. He filled that vacancy with this remark, uttered with tranquil complacency: "I've never read any of his books, on account of prejudice."

Before we had become fairly settled in the new quarters, Webster had suggested that we abolish the existing contract and make a new one. Very well, it was done. I probably never read it nor asked anybody else to read it. I probably merely signed it and saved myself further bother in that way. Under the preceding contracts Webster had been my paid servant; under the new one I was his slave, his absolute slave, and without salary. I owned nine-tenths of the business, I furnished all the capital, I shouldered all the losses, I was responsible for everything, but Webster was sole master. This new condition and my sarcasms changed the atmosphere. I could no longer give orders as before. I could not even make a suggestion with any considerable likelihood of its acceptance.

General Grant was a sick man but he wrought upon his memoirs like a well one and made steady and sure progress.

Webster throned himself in the rope walk and issued a summons to the sixteen general agents to come from the sixteen quarters of the United States and sign contracts. They came. They assembled. Webster delivered the law to them as from Mt. Sinai. They kept their temper wonderfully, marvelously. They furnished the bonds required. They signed the contracts and departed. Ordinarily they would have resented the young man's arrogances but this was not an ordinary case. The contracts were worth to each general agent a good many thousands of dollars. They knew this and the knowledge helped them to keep down their animosities.

Whitford was on hand. He was always at Webster's elbow. Webster was afraid to do anything without legal advice. He could have all the legal advice he wanted, because he had now hired Whitford by the year. He was paying him ten thousand dollars a year out of my pocket. And indeed Whitford was worth part of it—the two-hundredth part of it. It was the first time he had ever earned anything worth speaking of and he was content. The phrase "worth speaking of" is surplusage. Whitford had never earned anything. Whitford was never destined to earn anything. He did not earn the ten thousand dollars nor any part of it. In two instances his services proved a pecuniary damage to the firm. His other services were inconsequential and unnecessary. The bookkeeper could have performed them.

Whenever galley proofs or revises went to General

Grant, a set came also to me. General Grant was aware of this. Sometimes I referred to the proofs casually, but entered into no particulars concerning them. By and by I learned through a member of the household that he was disturbed and disappointed because I had never expressed an opinion as to the literary quality of the memoirs. It was also suggested that a word of encouragement from me would be a help to him. I was as much surprised as Columbus's cook could have been to learn that Columbus wanted his opinion as to how Columbus was doing his navigating. It could not have occurred to me that General Grant could have any use for anybody's assistance or encouragement in any work which he might undertake to do. He was the most modest of men and this was another instance of it. He was venturing upon a new trade, an uncharted sea, and stood in need of the encouraging word just like any creature of common clay. It was a great compliment that he should care for my opinion and should desire it, and I took the earliest opportunity to diplomatically turn the conversation in that direction and furnish it without seeming to lug it in by the ears.

By chance, I had been comparing the memoirs with Caesar's "Commentaries" and was qualified to deliver judgment. I was able to say in all sincerity that the same high merits distinguished both books—clarity of statement, directness, simplicity, unpretentiousness, manifest truthfulness, fairness and justice toward friend and foe alike, soldierly candor and frankness, and soldierly avoidance of flowery speech. I placed the two books side by side upon the same high level, and I still think that they belonged there. I learned afterward that General Grant was pleased with this verdict. It shows that he was just a man, just a human being, just an author. An author values a compliment even when it comes from a source of doubtful competency.

General Grant wrought heroically with his pen while his disease made its steady inroads upon his life, and at last his work stood completed. He was moved to Mount McGregor and there his strength passed gradually away. Toward the last he was not able to speak, but used a pencil and small slips of paper when he needed to say anything.

I went there to see him once toward the end, and he asked me with his pencil, and evidently with anxious solicitude, if there was a prospect that his book would make something for his family.

I said that the canvass for it was progressing vigorously, that the subscriptions and the money were coming in fast, that the campaign was not more than half completed yet—but that if it should stop where it was there would be two hundred thousand dollars coming to his family. He expressed his gratification, with his pencil.

When I was entering the house, the Confederate general, Buckner, was leaving it. Buckner and Grant had been fellow cadets at West Point, about 1840. I think they had served together in the Mexican war, a little later. After that war Grant (then a captain in the regular army) was ordered to a military post in Oregon. By and by he resigned and came East and found himself in New York penniless. On the street he met Buckner and borrowed fifty dollars of him. In February, 1862, Buckner was in command of the Confederate garrison of Fort Donelson. General Grant captured the fortress by assault and took fifteen thousand prisoners. After that, the two soldiers did not meet again until that day at Mount McGregor twenty-three years later.

Several visitors were present and there was a good deal of chaffing and joking, some of it at Buckner's expense.

Finally General Buckner said, "I have my full share of admiration and esteem for Grant. It dates back to our cadet days. He has as many merits and virtues as any man I am acquainted with but he has one deadly defect. He is an incurable borrower and when he wants to borrow he knows of only one limit—he wants what you've got. When I was poor he borrowed fifty dollars of me; when I was rich he borrowed fifteen thousand men."

General Grant died at Mount McGregor on the 23rd of July. In September or October the memoirs went to press. Several sets of plates were made; the printing was distributed among several great printing establishments; a great number of steam presses were kept running night and day on the book; several large binderies were kept at work binding it. The book was in sets of two volumes—large octavo. Its price was nine dollars in cloth. For costlier bindings the price was proportionately higher. Two thousand sets in tree-calf were issued at twenty-five dollars per set.

The book was issued on the 10th of December, and I turned out to be a competent prophet. In the beginning I had told General Grant that his book would sell six hundred thousand single volumes, and that is what happened. It sold three hundred thousand sets. The first check that went to Mrs. Grant was for two hundred thousand dollars; the next one, a few months later, was for a hundred and fifty thousand. I do not remember about the subsequent checks but I think that in the aggregate the book paid Mrs. Grant something like half a million dollars.

Webster was in his glory. In his obscure days his hat was number six and a quarter; in these latter days he was not able to get his head into a barrel. He loved to descant upon the wonders of the book. He liked to go into the statistics. He liked to tell that it took thirteen miles of gold leaf to print the gilt titles on the book backs; he liked to tell how many thousand tons the three hundred thousand sets weighed. Of course that same old natural thing happened: Webster thought it was *he* that sold the book. He thought that General Grant's great name helped but he regarded himself as the main reason of the book's prodigious success. This shows that Webster was merely human and merely a publisher. All publishers are Columbuses. The successful author is their America. The reflection that they—like Columbus—didn't discover what they expected to discover, and didn't discover what they started out to discover, doesn't trouble them. All they remember is that they discovered America; they forget that they started out to discover some patch or corner of India.

—1906

Failure of a Publisher

In the early days, when the general agents were being chosen, Webster conferred one of the best Western general agencies upon an ex-preacher, a professional revivalist whom God had deposited in Iowa for improprieties of one kind and another which had been committed by that State. All the other candidates for agencies warned Webster to keep out of that man's hands, assuring him that no sagacities of Whitford or anybody else would be able to defeat that revivalist's inborn proclivity to steal. Their persuasions went for nothing. Webster gave him the agency. We furnished him the books. He did a thriving trade. He collected a gross sum of thirty-six thousand dollars and Webster never got a cent of it.

It is no great marvel to me that Mrs. Grant got a matter of half a million dollars out of that book. The miracle is that it didn't run her into debt. It was fortunate for her that we had only one Webster. It was an unnatural oversight in me that I didn't hunt for another one.

Let me try to bring this painful business to a close. One of the things which poisoned Webster's days and nights was the aggravating circumstance that whereas he, Charles L. Webster, was the great publisher—the greatest of publishers—and my name did not appear anywhere as a member of the firm, the public persisted in regarding me as the substance of that firm and Webster the shadow. Everybody who had a book to publish offered it to me, not to Webster. I accepted several excellent books but Webster declined them every time, and he was master. But if anybody offered *him* a book, he was so charmed with the compliment that he took the book without examining it. He was not able to get hold of one that could make its living.

Joe Jefferson wrote me and said he had written his autobiography and he would like me to be the publisher. Of course I wanted the book. I sent his letter to Webster and asked him to arrange the matter. Webster did not decline the book. He simply ignored it and brushed the matter out of his mind. He accepted and published two or three war books that furnished no profit. He accepted still another one: distributed the agency contracts for it, named its price (three dollars and a half in cloth) and also agreed to have the book ready by a certain date, two or three months ahead. One day I went down to New York and visited the office and asked for a sight of that book. I asked Webster how many thousand words it contained. He said he didn't know. I asked him to count the words, by rough estimate. He did it. I said, "It doesn't contain words enough for the price and dimensions, by four-fifths. You will have to pad it with a brick. We must start a brickyard, and right away, because it is much cheaper to make bricks than it is to buy them in the market."

It set him in a fury. Any little thing like that would have that effect. He was one of the most sensitive creatures I ever saw, for the quality of the material that he was made of.

He had several books on hand—worthless books which he had accepted because they had been offered to him instead of to me—and I found that he had never counted the words in any of them. He had taken them without examination. Webster was a good general agent but he knew nothing about publishing, and he was incapable of learning anything about it. By and by I found that he had agreed to resurrect Henry Ward Beecher's *Life of Christ.* I suggested that he ought to have tried for Lazarus, because that had been tried once and we knew it could be done. He was exasperated again. He certainly was the most sensitive creature that ever was, for his make. He had also advanced to Mr. Beecher, who was not in prosperous circumstances at the time, five thousand dollars on the future royalties. Mr. Beecher was to revamp the book—or rather I think he was to finish the book. I think he had just issued the first of the two volumes of which it was to consist when that ruinous scandal broke out and suffocated the enterprise. I think the second volume had not been written and that Mr. Beecher was now undertaking to write it. If he failed to accomplish this within a given time he was to return the money. He did not succeed and the money was eventually returned.

Webster kept back a book of mine, *A Connecticut Yankee in King Arthur's Court,* as long as he could and finally published it so surreptitiously that it took two or three years to find out that there was any such book. He suppressed a compilation made by Howells and me, *The Library of Humor*, so long and finally issued it so clandestinely that I doubt if anybody in America ever did find out that there was such a book.

William M. Laffan told me that Mr. Walters, of Baltimore, was going to have a sumptuous book made which should illustrate in detail his princely art collection; that he was going to bring the best artists from Paris to make the illustrations; that he was going to make the book himself and see to it that it was made exactly to his taste; that he was going to spend a quarter of a million dollars on it; that he wanted it issued at a great price—a price consonant with its sumptuous character, and that he wanted no penny of the proceeds. The publisher would have nothing to do but distribute the book and take the whole of the profit.

Laffan said, "There, Mark, you can make a fortune out of that without any trouble at all, and without risk or expense."

I said I would send Webster down to Baltimore at once. I tried to do it but I never succeeded. Webster never touched the matter in any way whatever. If it had been a secondhand dog that Mr. Walters wanted published, he would have only needed to apply to Webster. Webster would have broken his neck getting down to Baltimore to annex that dog. But Mr. Walters had applied to the wrong man. Webster's pride was hurt and he would not look at Mr. Walters's book. Webster had immense pride but he was short of other talents.

Webster was the victim of a cruel neuralgia in the head. He eased his pain with the new German drug, phenacetine. The physicians limited his use of it but he found a way to get it in quantity: under our free institutions anybody can poison himself that wants to and will pay the price. He took this drug with increasing frequency and in increasing quantity. It stupefied him and he went about as one in a dream. He ceased from coming to the office except at intervals, and when he came he was pretty sure to exercise his authority in ways perilous for the business. In his condition, he was not responsible for his acts.

Something had to be done. Whitford explained that there was no way to get rid of this dangerous element except by buying Webster out. But what was there to buy? Webster had always promptly collected any money that was due him. He had squandered, long ago, my share of the book's profit—a hundred thousand dollars. The business was gasping, dying. The whole of it was not worth a dollar and a half. Then what would be a fair price for me to pay for a tenth interest in it? After much consultation and much correspondence, it transpired that Webster would be willing to put up with twelve thousand dollars and step out. I furnished the check.

Webster's understudy and business manager had now been for some time a young fellow named Frederick J. Hall, another Dunkirk importation. We got all our talent from that stud farm at Dunkirk. Poor Hall meant well but he was wholly incompetent for the place. He carried it along for a time with the heroic hopefulness of youth, but there was an obstruction which was bound to defeat him sooner or later. It was this:

Stedman, the poet, had made a compilation, several years earlier, called *The Library of American Literature*—nine or ten octavo volumes. A publisher in Cincinnati had tried to make it succeed. It swallowed up that publisher, family and all. If Stedman had offered me the book I should have said "Sold by subscription and on the installment plan, there is nothing in this book for us at a royalty above four per cent, but in fact it would swamp us at any kind of royalty, because such a book would require a cash capital of several hundred thousand dollars, and we haven't a hundred thousand."

But Stedman didn't bring the book to me. He took it to Webster. Webster was delighted and flattered. He accepted the book on an eight per cent royalty, and thereby secured the lingering suicide of Charles L. Webster and Company. We struggled along two or three years under that deadly load. After Webster's time, poor little Hall struggled along with it and got to borrowing money of a bank in which Whitford was a director—borrowing on notes endorsed by me and renewed from time to time. These notes used to come to me in Italy for renewals. I endorsed them without examining them and sent them back. At last I found that additions had been made to the borrowings, without my knowledge or consent. I began to feel troubled. I wrote Mr. Hall about it and said I would like to have an exhaustive report of the condition of the business. The next mail brought that exhaustive report, whereby it appeared that the concern's assets exceeded its liabilities by ninety-two thousand dollars. Then I felt better. But there was no occasion to feel better, for the report ought to have read the other way. Poor Hall soon wrote to say that we needed more money and must have it right away or the concern would fail.

I sailed for New York. I emptied into the till twenty-four thousand dollars which I had earned with the pen. I looked around to see where we could borrow money. There wasn't any place. This was in the midst of the fearful panic of '93. I went up to Hartford to borrow—couldn't borrow a penny. I offered to mortgage our house and grounds and furniture for any small loan. The property had cost a hundred and sixty-seven thousand dollars, and seemed good for a small loan. Henry Robinson said, "Clemens, I give you my word, you can't borrow three thousand dollars on that property." Very well, I knew that if that was so, I couldn't borrow it on a basketful of government bonds.

Webster and Company failed. The firm owed me about sixty thousand dollars, borrowed money. It owed Mrs. Clemens sixty-five thousand dollars, borrowed money. Also it owed ninety-six creditors an average of a thousand dollars or so apiece. The panic had stopped Mrs. Clemens's income. It had stopped my income from my books. We had but nine thousand dollars in the bank. We hadn't a penny wherewith to pay the Webster creditors. Henry Robinson said, "Hand over everything belonging to Webster and Company to the creditors, and ask them to accept that in liquidation of the debts. They'll do it. You'll see that they'll do it. They are aware that you are not individually responsible for those debts, that the responsibility rests upon the firm as a firm."

I didn't think much of that way out of the difficulty and when I made my report to Mrs. Clemens she wouldn't hear of it at all. She said, "This is my house. The creditors shall have it. Your books are your property—turn them over to the creditors. Reduce the indebtedness in every way you can think of—then get to work and earn the rest of the indebtedness, if your life is spared. And don't be afraid. We shall pay a hundred cents on the dollar yet."

It was sound prophecy. Mr. Rogers stepped in, about this time, and preached to the creditors. He said they could not have Mrs. Clemens's house—that she must be a preferred creditor and would give up the Webster notes for sixty-five thousand dollars, money borrowed of her. He said they could not have my books, that they were not an asset of Webster and Company, that the creditors could have everything that belonged to Webster and Company, that I would wipe from the slate the sixty thousand dollars I had lent to the Company, and that I would now make it my task to earn the rest of the Webster indebtedness, if I could, and pay a hundred cents on the dollar—but that this must not be regarded as a promise.

In a conversation with Mr. Rogers and a couple of lawyers, in those days, one of the men said, "Not five per cent of the men who become ruined at fifty-eight ever recover." Another said, with enthusiasm, "Five per cent! None of them ever recovers." It made me feel very sick.

That was in '94, I believe—though it may have been in the beginning of '95. However, Mrs. Clemens and Clara and I started, on the 15th of July, 1985, on our lecturing raid around the world. We lectured and robbed and raided for thirteen months. I wrote a book and published it. I sent the book money and lecture money to Mr. Rogers as fast as we captured it. He banked it and saved it up for the creditors. We implored him to pay off the smaller creditors straightway, for they needed the money, but he wouldn't do it. He said that when I had milked the world dry we would take the result and distribute it *pro rata* among the Webster people.

At the end of '98 or the beginning of '99 Mr. Rogers cabled me, at Vienna, "The creditors have all been paid a hundred cents on the dollar. There is eighteen thousand five hundred dollars left. What shall I do with it?"

I answered, "Put it in Federal Steel"—which he did, all except a thousand dollars, and took it out again in two months with a profit of a hundred and twenty-five per cent.

There—Thanks be! A hundred times I have tried to tell this intolerable story with a pen, but I never could do it. It always made me sick before I got halfway to the middle of it. But this time I have held my grip and walked the floor and emptied it all out of my system, and I hope to never hear of it again.

—1906

Private History of a Manuscript That Came to Grief

It happened in London; not recently, and yet not very many years ago. An acquaintance had proposed to himself a certain labor of love, and when he told me about it I was interested. His idea was to have a fine translation made of the evidence given in the *Joan of Arc Trials and Rehabilitation*, and placed before the English-speaking world. A translation had been made and published a great many years before, but had achieved no currency, and in fact was not entitled to any, for it was a piece of mere shoemaker-work. But we should have the proper thing, now; for this acquaintance of mine was manifestly a Joan enthusiast, and as he had plenty of money and nothing to do but spend it, I took at par his remark that he had employed the most competent person in Great Britain to open this long-neglected mine and confer its riches upon the public. When he asked me to write an Introduction for the book, my pleasure was complete, my vanity satisfied.

At this moment, by good fortune, there chanced to fall into my hands a biographical sketch of me of so just and laudatory a character—particularly as concerned one detail—that it gave my spirit great contentment; and also set my head to swelling—I will not deny it. For it contained praises of the very thing which I most loved to hear praised—*the good quality of my English*; moreover, they were uttered by four English and American literary experts of high authority.

I am as fond of compliments as another, and as hard to satisfy as the average; but these satisfied me. I was as pleased as you would have been if they had been paid to you.

It was under the inspiration of that great several-voiced verdict that I set about that Introduction for Mr. X's book; and I said to myself that I would put a quality of English into it which would establish the righteousness of that judgment. I said I would treat the subject with the reverence and dignity due it; and would use plain, simple English words, and a phrasing undefiled by meretricious artificialities and affectations.

I did the work on those lines; and when it was finished I said to myself very privately . . .

But never mind. I delivered the manuscript to Mr. X, and went home to wait for the praises. On the way I met a friend. Being in a happy glow over this pleasant matter, I could not keep my secret. I wanted to tell somebody, and I told him. For a moment he stood curiously measuring me up and down with his eye, without saying anything; then he burst into a rude, coarse laugh, which hurt me very much. He followed this up by saying:

"*He* is going to edit the translations of the *Trials* when it is finished? *He*?"

"He said he would."

"Why, what does he know about editing?"

"I don't know; but that is what he said. Do you think he isn't competent?"

"Competent? He is innocent, vain, ignorant, good-hearted, red-headed, and all that—there isn't a better-meaning man; but he doesn't know anything about literature and has had no literary training or experience; *he* can't edit anything."

"Well, all I know is, he is going to try."

"Indeed he will! He is quite unconscious of his incapacities; he would undertake to edit Shakespeare, if invited—and improve him, too. The world cannot furnish his match for guileless self-complacency; yet I give you my word he doesn't know enough to come in when it rains."

This gentleman's ability to judge was not to be questioned. Therefore, by the time I reached home I had concluded to ask Mr. X not to edit the translation, but to turn that work over to some expert whose name on the title page would be valuable.

Three days later Mr. X brought my Introduction to me, neatly typecopied. He was in a state of considerable enthusiasm, and said:

"Really I find it quite good—quite, I assure you."

There was an airy and patronizing complacency about this damp compliment which affected my head and healthfully checked the swelling which was going on there.

I said, with cold dignity, that I was glad the work had earned his approval.

"Oh, it has, I assure you!" he answered, with large cheerfulness. "I assure you it quite has. I have gone over it very thoroughly, yesterday and last night and to-day, and I find it quite creditable—quite. I have made a few corrections—that is, suggestions, and——"

"Do you mean to say that you have been ed——"

"Oh, nothing of consequence, nothing of consequence, I assure you," he said, patting me on the shoulder and genially smiling; "only a few little things that needed just a mere polishing touch—nothing of consequence, I assure you. Let me have it back as soon as you can, so that I can pass it on to the printers and let them get to work on it while I am editing the translation."

I sat idle and alone, a time, thinking grieved thoughts,

with the edited Introduction unopened in my hand. I could not look at it yet awhile. I had no heart for it, for my pride was deeply wounded. It was the only time I had been edited in thirty-two years, except by Mr. Howells, and he did not intrude his help, but furnished it at my request. "And now here is a half-stranger, obscure, destitute of literary training, destitute of literary experience, destitute of——"

But I checked myself there; for that way lay madness. I must seek calm; for my self-respect's sake I must not descend to unrefined personalities. I must keep in mind that this person was innocent of injurious intent and was honorably trying to do me a service. To feel harshly toward him, speak harshly of him—this was not the right Christian spirit. These just thoughts tranquillized me and restored to me my better self, and I opened the Introduction at the middle.

I will not deny it, my feelings rose to 104 in the shade:

"The idea! That his long-eared animal—this literary kangaroo—this illiterate hostler, with his skull full of axle grease—this . . ."

But I stopped there, for this was not the right Christian spirit.

I subjected myself to an hour of calming meditation, then carried the raped Introduction to that friend whom I have mentioned above and showed it to him. He fluttered the leaves over, then broke into another of those ill-bred laughs which are such a mar to him.

"I knew he would!" he said—as if gratified. "Didn't I tell you he would edit Shakespeare?"

"Yes, I know; but I did not suppose he would edit *me*."

"Oh, you didn't! Well, now you see that he is even equal to *that*. I tell you there are simply no bounds to that man's irreverence."

"I realize it, now," I said.

"Well, what are you going to do? Let him put it in his book—either edited or *un*edited?"

"Of course not!"

"That is well. You are becoming rational again. But what are your plans? You are not going to stop where you are, are you? You will write him a letter and give him Hark from the Tomb?"

"No, I shall write him a letter, but not in that spirit, I trust."

"*Why* shan't you?"

"Because he has meant me a kindness, and I hope I am not the man to reward him for it in that way."

The friend looked me over awhile, pensively, then said——

"Mark, I am ashamed of you. This is mere school-girl sentimentality. You ought to baste him—you know it yourself."

I said I had no such feeling in my heart and should put nothing of the kind in my letter.

"I shall point out his errors to him in gentleness and in the unwounding language of persuasion. Many a literary beginner has been disheartened and defeated by the uncharitable word wantonly uttered; this one shall get none such from me. It is more Christian-like to do a good turn than an ill one, and you ought to encourage me in my attitude, not scoff at it. This man shall not be my enemy; I will make him my lasting and grateful friend."

I felt that I was in the right, and I went home and began the letter and found pleasure and contentment in the labor, for I had the encouragement and support of an approving conscience.

The letter will be found in its proper place in this chapter of my *Autobiography*; it follows:

The Letter

Dear Mr. X:

I find on my desk the first two pages of Miss Z's translation, with your emendations marked in them. Thank you for sending them.

I have examined the first page of my amended Introduction and will begin now and jot down some notes upon your corrections. If I find any changes which shall not seem to me to be improvements, I will point out my reasons for thinking so. In this way I may chance to be helpful to you and thus profit you, perhaps, as much as you have desired to profit me.

Notes

Section I. *First Paragraph.* "Jeanne d'Arc." This is rather cheaply pedantic, and is not in very good taste. Joan is not known by that name among plain people of our race and tongue. I notice that the name of the Deity occurs several times in the brief installment of the *Trials* which you have favored me with; to be consistent, it will be necessary that you strike out "God" and put in "Dieu." Do not neglect this.

First line. What is the trouble with "*at the*"? And why "*Trial*?" Has some uninstructed person deceived you into the notion that there was but one, instead of half a dozen?

Amongst. Wasn't "*among*" good enough?

Next half-dozen Corrections. Have you failed to perceive that by taking the word "*both*" out of its proper place you have made foolishness of the sentence? And don't you see that your smug "*of which*" has turned *that* sentence into reporter's English? "*Quite.*" Why do you intrude that shopworn favorite of yours where there is nothing useful for it to do? Can't you rest easy in your literary grave without it?

Next sentence. You have made no improvement in it. Did you change it merely to *be* changing something?

Second Paragraph. Now you have begun on my punctuation. Don't you realize that you ought not to intrude your help in a delicate art like that, with your limitations? And do you think you have added just the right smear of polish to the closing clause of the sentence?

Second Paragraph. How do you know it was his "own" sword? It could have been a borrowed one. I am cautious in matters of history, and you should not put statements in my mouth for which you cannot produce vouchers. Your other corrections are rubbish.

Third Paragraph. Ditto.

Fourth Paragraph. Your word "directly" is misleading; it could be construed to mean "at once." Plain clarity is better than ornate obscurity. I note your sensitive marginal remark: "*Rather unkind to French feelings—referring to Moscow.*" Indeed, I have not been concerning myself about French feelings, but only about stating the facts. I have said several uncourteous things about the French—calling them a "nation of ingrates," in one place—but you have been so busy editing commas and semicolons that you overlooked them and failed to get scared at them. The next paragraph ends with a slur at the French, but I have reasons for thinking you mistook it for a compliment. It is discouraging to try to penetrate a mind like yours. You ought to get it out and dance on it. That would take some of the rigidity out of it. And you ought to use it sometimes; that would help. If you had done this every now and then along through life, it would not have petrified.

Fifth Paragraph. Thus far, I regard this as your masterpiece! Your are really perfect in the great art of reducing simple and dignified speech to clumsy and vapid commonplace.

Sixth Paragraph. You have a singularly fine and aristocratic disrespect for homely and unpretending English. Every time I use "go back" you get out your polisher and slick it up to "return." "Return" is suited only to the drawing-room—it is ducal, and says itself with a simper and a smirk.

Seventh Paragraph. "Permission" is dual. Ducal and affected. "Her" great days were *not* "over"; they were only half over. Didn't you know that? Haven't you read anything at all about Joan of Arc? The truth is, you do not pay any attention; I told you on my very first page that the public part of her career lasted two years, and you have forgotten it already. You really must get your mind out and have it repaired; you see, yourself, that it is all caked together.

Eighth Paragraph. She "rode away *to* assault and capture a stronghold." Very well; but you do not tell us whether she succeeded or not. You should not worry the reader with uncertainties like that. I will remind you once more that clarity is a good thing in literature. An apprentice cannot do better than keep this useful rule in mind.

Closing Sentences. Corrections which are not corrections.

Ninth Paragraph. "Known" history. That word is a polish which is too delicate for me; there doesn't seem to be any sense in it. This would have surprised me, last week.

Second Sentence. It cost me an hour's study before I found out what it meant. I see, now, that it is intended to mean what it meant before. It really does accomplish its intent, I think, though in a most intricate and slovenly fashion. What was your idea in reframing it? Merely in order that you might add this to your other editorial contributions and be able to say to people that the most of the Introduction was your work? I am afraid that that was really your sly and unparliamentary scheme. Certainly we do seem to live in a very wicked world.

Closing Sentence. There is your empty "however" again. I cannot think what makes you so flatulent.

II. *In Captivity.* "Remainder." It is curious and interesting to notice what an attraction a fussy, mincing, nickel-plated artificial word has for you. This is not well.

Third Sentence. But she *was* held to ransom; it wasn't a case of "should have been" and it wasn't a case of "*if* it had been offered"; it *was* offered, and also accepted, as the second paragraph shows. You ought never to edit except when awake.

Fourth Sentence. Why do you wish to change that? It was more than "demanded"; it was *required.* Have you no sense of shades of meaning in words?

Fifth Sentence. Changing it to "benefactress" takes the dignity out of it. If I had called her a braggart, I suppose you would have polished her into a braggartess, with your curious and random notions about the English tongue.

Closing Sentence. "Sustained" is sufficiently nickel-plated to meet the requirements of your disease, I trust. "Wholly" adds nothing; the sentence means just what it meant before. In the rest of the sentence you sacrifice simplicity to airy fussiness.

Second Paragraph. It was not blood money, unteachable ass, any more than is the money that buys a house or a horse; it was an ordinary business transaction of the time, and was not dishonorable. "With her hands, feet and neck *both* chained," etc. The restricted word "both" cannot be applied to three things, but only to two. "*Fence*:" You "lifted" that word from further along—and with what valuable result? The next sentence—after your doctoring of it—has no meaning. The one succeeding it—after your doctoring of it—refers to nothing, wanders around in space, has no meaning and no reason for existing, and is by a shade or two more demented and twaddlesome than anything hitherto ground out of your strange and interesting editorial mill.

Closing Sentence. "Neither" for "either." Have you now debauched the grammar to your taste?

Third Paragraph. It was sound English before you decayed it. Sell it to the museum.

Fourth Paragraph. I note the compliment you pay yourself, margined opposite the closing sentence: "*Easier translation.*" But it has two defects. In the first place it is a *mis*translation, and in the second place it translates half of the grace out of Joan's remark.

Fifth Paragraph. Why are you so prejudiced against fact and so indecently fond of fiction? Her generalship was *not* "that of a tried and trained military experience," for she hadn't had any, and no one swore that she had had any. I had stated the facts; you should have reserved your fictions.

Note: To be intelligible, that whole paragraph must consist of a single sentence; in breaking it up into several, you have knocked the sense all out of it.

Eighth Paragraph. "When the flames leapt up and enveloped her frail form" is handsome, very handsome, even elegant, but it isn't yours; you hooked it out of "The Costermonger's Bride; or The Fire Fiend's Foe." To take other people's things is not right, and God will punish you. "*Parched*" lips? How do you know they were? Why do you make statements which you cannot verify, when you have no motive for it but to work in a word which you think is nobby?

III. *The Rehabilitation.* "Their statements were taken down *as evidence.*" Wonderful! If you had failed to mention that particular, many persons might have thought they were taken down as entertainment.

IV. *The Riddle of All Time.* I note your marginal remark: "Riddle—Anglice?" Look in your spelling book. "We can understand how the genius was created," etc., "by steady and congenial growth." We can't understand anything of the kind; genius is not "created" by any farming process—it is *born*. You are thinking of potatoes. *Note:* Whenever I say "circumstances" you change it to "environment"; and you persistently change my thats into whiches and my whiches into thats. This is merely silly, you know.

Second Paragraph. I note your marginal remark, "*2 comprehends.*" I suppose some one has told you that repetition is tautology, and then has left you to believe that repetition is always tautology. But let it go; with your limitations one would not be able to teach you how to distinguish between the repetition which isn't tautology and the repetition which is.

Closing Sentence. Your tipsy emendation, when straightened up on its legs and examined, is found to say this: "We fail to see her issue thus equipped, and we cannot understand why." That is to say, she did *not* issue so equipped, and you cannot make out why she didn't. *That* is the riddle that defeats you, labor at it as you may? Why, if that had happened, it wouldn't be a riddle at all—except to you—but a thing likely to happen to nearly anybody, and not matter for astonishment to any intelligent person standing by at the time—or later. There *is* a riddle, but you have mistaken the nature of it, I cannot tell how, labor at it as I may; and I will try to point it out to you so that you can see some of it. We do *not* fail to see her issue so equipped, we *do* see her. That is the whole marvel, mystery, riddle. That she, an ignorant country girl, sprang upon the world equipped with amazing natural gifts is not the riddle—it could have happened to you if you had been some one else; but the fact that those talents were instantly and effectively usable *without previous training* is the mystery which we cannot master, the riddle which we cannot solve. Do you get it?

Third Paragraph. Drunk.

V. *As Prophet.* "And in *every case* realized the complete fulfillment." How do you know she did that? There is no testimony to back up that wild assertion. I was particular not to claim that all her prophecies came true; for that would have been to claim that we have her whole list, whereas it is likely that she made some that failed and did not get upon the record. People do not record prophecies that failed. Such is not the custom.

VI. *Her Character.* "Comforted" is a good change, and quite sane. But you are not playing fair; you are getting some sane person to help you. *Note:* When I wrote "counselled her, advised her," *that* was tautology; the "2 comprehends" was a case of repetition which was *not* tautological. But I am sure you will never be able to learn the difference. *Note:* "But she, Jeanne d'Arc, when presently she found," etc. That is the funniest yet, and the commonplacest. But it isn't original, you got it out of "How to Write Literary Without Any

Apprenticeship," sixpence to the trade; retail, sevenpence farthing. *Erased Passage.* I note with admiration your marginal remark explaining your objection to it: "*Is it warrantable to assert that she bragged? Is it in good taste? It was assuredly foreign to her character.*" I will admit that my small effort at playfulness was not much of a pearl, but such as it was, I realize that I threw it into the wrong trough.

VII. *Her Face and Form.* You have misunderstood me again. I did not mean that the artist had several ideas and one prevailing one; I meant that he had only *one* idea. In that same sentence, "omits" and "forgets" have just the same meaning; have you any clear idea, then, why you made the change? Is it your notion that "gross" is an improvement on "big," "perform" an improvement on "do," "inquiring" an improvement on "asking," and "in such wise" an improvement on "then," or have you merely been seduced by the fine, large sounds of those words? Are you incurably hostile to simplicity of speech? And finally, do you not see that you have edited all the dignity out of the paragraph and substituted simpering commonplace for it, and that your addition at the end is a deliciously flat and funny anticlimax? Still I note your command in the margin, "*Insert this remark*," and I dutifully obey.

Second Paragraph. "Exploited" was worth a shilling, there; you have traded it for a word not worth tuppence ha'-penny, and got cheated, and serves you right. Read "rightly," if it shocks you.

Close of Paragraph. You have exploited another anti-climax—and in the form, too, of an impudent advertisement of your book. It seems to me that for a person of your elegance of language you are curiously lacking in certain other delicacies.

Third Paragraph. I must reserve my thanks. "Moreover" is a parenthesis, when interjected in that fashion; a parenthesis is evidence that the man who uses it does not know how to write English or is too indolent to take the trouble to do it; a parenthesis usually throws the emphasis upon the wrong word, and has done it in this instance; a man who will wantonly use a parenthesis will steal. For these reasons I am unfriendly to the parenthesis. When a man puts one into my mouth his life is no longer safe. "Break another lance" is a knightly and sumptuous phrase, and I honor it for its hoary age and for the faithful service it has done in the prize-composition of the schoolgirl, but I have ceased from employing it since I got my puberty, and must solemnly object to fathering it here. And besides, it makes me hint that I have broken one of those things before, in honor of the Maid, an intimation not justified by the facts. I did not break any lances or other furniture, I only wrote a book about her.

Truly yours,

MARK TWAIN.

It cost me something to restrain myself and say these smooth and half-flattering things to this immeasurable idiot, but I did it and have never regretted it. For it is higher and nobler to be kind to even a shad like him than just. If we should deal out justice only, in this world, who would escape? No, it is better to be generous, and in the end more profitable, for it gains gratitude for us, and love, and it is far better to have the love of a literary strumpet like this than the reproaches of his wounded spirit. Therefore I am glad I said no harsh things to him, but spared him, the same as I would a tapeworm. It is reward enough for me to know that my children will be proud of their father for this, when I am gone. I could have said hundreds of unpleasant things about this tadpole, but I did not even feel them.

—1900

A Helpless Situation

Once or twice a year I get a letter of a certain pattern, a pattern that never materially changes, in form and substance, yet I cannot get used to that letter—it always astonishes me. It affects me as the locomotive always affects me: I say to myself, "I have seen you a thousand times, you always look the same way, yet you are always a wonder, and you are always impossible; to contrive you is clearly beyond human genius—you can't exist, you don't exist, yet here you are!"

I have a letter of that kind by me, a very old one. I yearn to print it, and where is the harm? The writer of it is dead years ago, no doubt, and if I conceal her name and address—her this-world address—I am sure her shade will not mind. And with it I wish to print the answer which I wrote at the time but probably did not send. If it went—which is not likely—it went in the form of a copy, for I find the original still here, pigeonholed with the said letter. To that kind of letter we all write answers which we do not send, fearing to hurt where we have no desire to hurt; I have done it many a time, and this is doubtless a case of the sort.

THE LETTER

X———., *CALIFORNIA, June 3, 1879.*

MR. S. L. CLEMENS, Hartford, Conn.:

DEAR SIR,—You will doubtless be surprised to know who has presumed to write and ask a favor of you. Let your memory go back to your days in the Humboldt mines—'62-'63. You will remember, you and Clagett and Oliver and the old blacksmith Tillou lived in a lean-to which was half-way up the gulch, and there were six log cabins in the camp—strung pretty well separated up the gulch from its mouth at the desert to where the last claim was, at the divide. The lean-to you lived in was the one with a canvas roof that the cow fell down through one night, as told about by you in *Roughing It*—my uncle Simmons remembers it very well. He lived in the principal cabin, half-way up the divide, along with Dixon and Parker and Smith. It had two rooms, one for kitchen and the other for bunks, and was the only one that had. You and your party were there on the great night, the time they had dried-apple-pie, Uncle Simmons often speaks of it. It seems curious that dried-apple-pie should have seemed such a great thing, but it was, and it shows how far Humboldt was out of the world and difficult to get to, and how slim the regular bill of fare was. Sixteen years ago—it is a long time. I was a little girl then, only fourteen. I never saw you, I lived in Washoe. But Uncle Simmons ran across you every now and then, all during those weeks that you and party were there working your claim which was like the rest. The camp played out long and long ago, there wasn't silver enough in it to make a button. You never saw my husband, but he was there after you left, *and lived in that very lean-to*, a bachelor then but married to me now. He often wishes there had been a photographer there in those days, he would have taken the lean-to. He got hurt in the old Hal Clayton claim that was abandoned like the others, putting in a blast and not climbing out quick enough, though he scrambled the best he could. It landed him clear down on the trail and hit a Piute. For weeks they thought he would not get over it but he did, and is all right, now. Has been ever since. This is a long introduction but it is the only way I can make myself known. The favor I ask I feel assured your generous heart will grant: Give me some advice about a book I have written. I do not claim anything for it only it is mostly true and as interesting as most of the books of the times. I am unknown in the literary world and you know what that means unless one has some one of influence (like yourself) to help you by speaking a good word for you. I would like to place the book on royalty basis plan with any one you would suggest.

This is a secret from my husband and family. I intend it as a surprise in case I get it published.

Feeling you will take an interest in this and if possible write me a letter to some publisher, or, better still, if you could see them for me and then let me hear.

I appeal to you to grant me this favor. With deepest gratitude I thank you for your attention.

One knows, without inquiring, that the twin of that embarrassing letter is forever and ever flying in this and that and the other direction across the continent in the mails, daily, nightly, hourly, unceasingly, unrestingly. It goes to every well-known merchant, and railway official, and manufacturer, and capitalist, and Mayor, and Congressman, and Governor, and editor, and publisher, and author, and broker, and banker—in a word, to every person who is supposed to have "influence." It always follows the one pattern: "*You do not know me, but you once knew a relative of mine*," etc., etc. We should all like to help the applicants, we should all be glad to do it, we should all like to return the sort of answer that is desired, but— Well, there is not a thing we can do that would be a help, for not in any instance does that letter ever come from anyone who *can* be helped. The struggler whom you *could* help does his own helping; it would not occur to him to apply to you, a stranger. He has talent and knows it, and he goes into his fight eagerly and with energy and determination—all alone, preferring to be alone. That pathetic letter which comes to you from the incapable, the unhelpable—how do you who are familiar with it answer it? What do you find to say? You do not want to inflict a wound; you hunt ways to avoid that. What do you find? How do you get out of your hard place with a contented conscience? Do you try to explain? The old reply of mine to such a letter shows that I tried that once. Was I satisfied with the result? Possibly; and possibly not; probably not; almost certainly not. I have long ago forgotten all about it. But, anyway, I append my effort:

The Reply

I know Mr. H., and I will go to him, dear madam, if upon reflection you find you still desire it. There will be a conversation. I know the form it will take. It will be like this:

Mr. H. How do her books strike you?
Mr. Clemens. I am not acquainted with them.
H. Who has been her publisher?
C. I don't know.
H. She *has* one, I suppose?
C. I—I think not.
H. Ah. You think this is her first book?
C. Yes—I suppose so. I think so.
H. What is it about? What is the character of it?
C. I believe I do not know.
H. Have you seen it?
C. Well—no, I haven't.
H. Ah-h. How long have you known her?
C. I don't know her.
H. Don't know her?
C. No.
H. Ah-h. How did you come to be interested in her book, then?
C. Well, she—she wrote and asked me to find a publisher for her, and mentioned you.
H. Why should she apply to you instead of to me?
C. She wished me to use my influence.
H. Dear me, what has *influence* to do with such a matter?
C. Well, I think she thought you would be more likely to examine her book if you were influenced.

H. Why, what we are here *for* is to examine books—anybody's book that comes along. It's our *business.* Why should we turn away a book unexamined because it's a stranger's? It would be foolish. No publisher does it. On what ground did she request your influence, since you do not know her? She must have thought you knew her literature and could speak for it. Is that it?

C. No; she knew I didn't.

H. Well, what then? She had a reason of *some* sort for believing you competent to recommend her literature, and also under obligations to do it?

C. Yes, I—I knew her uncle.

H. Knew her *uncle?*

C. Yes.

H. Upon my word! So, you knew her uncle; her uncle knows her literature; he indorses it to you; the chain is complete, nothing further needed; you are satisfied, and therefore—

C. No, that isn't all, there are other ties. I know the cabin her uncle lived in, in the mines; I knew his partners, too; also I came near knowing her husband before she married him, and I *did* know the abandoned shaft where a premature blast went off and he went flying through the air and clear down to the trail and hit an Indian in the back with almost fatal consequences.

H. To *him*, or to the Indian?

C. She didn't say which it was.

H. (*With a sigh*). It certainly beats the band! You don't know *her,* you don't know her literature, you don't know who got hurt when the blast went off, you don't know a single thing for us to build an estimate of her book upon, so far as I—

C. I knew her uncle. You are forgetting her uncle.

H. Oh, what use is *he?* Did you know him long?

How long was it?

C. Well, I don't know that I really knew him, but I must have met him, anyway. I think it was that way; you can't tell about these things, you know, except when they are recent.

H. Recent? When was all this?

C. Sixteen years ago.

H. What a basis to judge a book upon! At first you said you knew him, and now you don't know whether you did or not.

C. Oh yes, I knew him; anyway, I think I thought I did; I'm perfectly certain of it.

H. What makes you think you thought you knew him?

C. Why, she says I did, herself.

H. *She* says so!

C. Yes, she does, and I *did* know him, too, though I don't remember it now.

H. Come—how can you know it when you don't remember it.

C. I don't know. That is, I don't know the process, but I *do* know lots of things that I don't remember, and remember lots of things that I don't know. It's so with every educated person.

H. (*After a pause.*) Is your time valuable?

C. No—well, not very.

H. Mine is.

So I came away then, because he was looking tired. Overwork, I reckon; I never do that; I have seen the evil effects of it. My mother was always afraid I would overwork myself, but I never did.

Dear madam, you see how it would happen if I went there. He would ask me those questions, and I would try to answer them to suit him, and he would hunt me here and there and yonder and get me embarrassed more and more all the time, and at last he would look tired on account of overwork, and there it would end and nothing done. I wish I could be useful to you, but, you see, they do not care for uncles or any of those things; it doesn't move them, it doesn't have the least effect, they don't care for anything but the literature itself, and they as good as despise influence. But they do care for books, and are eager to get them and examine them, no matter whence they come, nor from whose pen. If you will send yours to a publisher—any publisher—he will certainly examine it, I can assure you of that.